NBA Jam

T0096905

NBA Jam

Reyan Ali

Boss Fight Books
Los Angeles, CA
bossfightbooks.com

Copyright © 2019 Reyan Ali
All rights reserved.

ISBN 13: 978-1-940535-20-3
First Printing: 2019

Series Editor: Gabe Durham
Associate Editor: Michael P. Williams
Book Design by Cory Schmitz
Page Design by Christopher Moyer

For Catalina

CONTENTS

PROLOGUE:
ATTRACT MODE

SOMEWHERE ALONG THE MAROON CARPET, between the mirrored walls, among the rows of gleaming screens that lit the room, you could find it: a crisp new arcade cabinet, moments away from debuting tonight at Dennis' Place for Games in Chicago, Illinois.

Standing at a height of 6′1″ and weighing in at 402 pounds, the machine was roughly the size of a refrigerator. Printed on the game's two sides were the pebbled orange pattern of a basketball, the silhouetted logo of the National Basketball Association, and the name "Midway" in fire hydrant red italics. The device contained two coin slots, four control stations, a powerful speaker system, and a 25-inch cathode ray tube monitor built to shine night and day. A marquee at the top of the machine announced the name of the game in all caps: *NBA JAM*.

But on this early evening in late 1992, those letters sat unlit, the machine still unpowered because *NBA Jam* was lacking a vital component: the erasable programmable read-only memory (EPROM) chip containing the latest version of the game's code. That piece of hardware was sitting a few miles away from the arcade on a desk at Williams Bally/Midway.

A titan in the coin-operated ("coin-op") video and pinball game industries, Williams Bally/Midway occupied a chunk of industrial real estate on Chicago's northwest side. In one massive facility, the company designed and programmed the software for their games, soldered the circuit boards, burned the memory chips, wired the electrical components, manufactured and decorated the games' wooden bodies (or "cabinets"), and did everything else in between. Games were boxed up and rolled out of their factory doors to arcades across the globe. The company went by several names (longtime employees called the operation Williams), but the world would come to know it best as Midway.

After spending the better part of a year programming and tweaking—endlessly, constantly *tweaking*—their high-energy take on virtual basketball, the *NBA Jam* team just had a few more last-minute adjustments to make. Once everything was ready, the freshest revision of the code was burned to an EPROM chip, then picked up and taken out the door. *NBA Jam* was about to move from the comfortable confines of the Midway office to the wilderness of public opinion.

When a coin-op was almost complete, Midway would send a cabinet or two out "on location" or "on test" to a local arcade to get an idea of how the game would perform upon wide release and how many cabinets to build. Chicago was dotted with places ripe for candid customer feedback. A few months earlier, Midway had placed a fighting game called *Mortal Kombat* in the nearby Times Square Arcade. The game was now on its way to catapulting Midway to record earnings, and *NBA Jam* had the makings of a hit, too.

Tonight, *Jam*'s future lay in the hands of the patrons of Dennis' Place for Games at 957 West Belmont Avenue. All sorts came through Dennis' doors: hardcore gamers and schoolchildren, teens and families, hipsters and gangsters alike.

Tucked into a corner building across from the Belmont Red Line "L" stop, Dennis' Place was easily spotted by its big sign dotted with light bulbs. In an oval on the sign, a young man in uniform with a shock of neatly parted red hair stared stoically. He was illustrated from the shoulders up, seeming as if he was posing for a military portrait. The logo was traditional and trustworthy, the kind of old-world insignia you could throw on a bottle of aftershave or a jar of pasta sauce without a second thought.

The man on the sign and on the arcade's tokens was Dennis Georges. Born and raised in Greece, where he served in the navy, Georges dreamed of immigrating to America and starting a business. Arriving in the early 1960s, he eventually found his calling in the booming storefront video game arcade industry and opened Dennis' Place for Games in the late 70s. Over the years, Georges expanded the business into multiple locations, but this spot—the one on West Belmont—was the *real* one.

A black belt in karate and former pro boxer, Georges was friendly but no-nonsense when it came to the rules. His game rooms prohibited smoking, drinking, eating, loitering, and wearing hats or head coverings. Because of a previous robbery, Georges suspended security cameras and microphones from the ceiling of the arcade and kept watch over his customers with a set of monitors in a back room.

Despite its touches of respectability, Dennis' Place had a habit of being dirty. Located in a rough and heavily trafficked part of Chicago, the arcade made a good spot to keep kids off the streets as the city's murder rate skyrocketed. Homeless youth and latchkey kids would pack the room long past midnight, staying warm in the machines' fluorescent glow.

For Midway's developers, visiting your game for its first night on test was a must. The set-up was win-win for everyone. Georges would reap the buzz of a new attraction appearing at his business (as well as the money the game generated). The *NBA Jam* team would look out for bugs, get to see how their work held up under public scrutiny, and have the opportunity to hang out with and cheer on their friends. Their lineup on opening night included, among others: *NBA Jam* team members Mark Turmell, Sal DiVita, John Carlton, and Jon Hey; *Terminator 2: Judgment Day* programmer George Petro; and *Defender* and *Robotron: 2084* designer Eugene Jarvis.

Eugene Jarvis's credentials, insight, and enthusiasm made him Midway's guiding star and one of the company's most deeply respected voices. He adored playing coin-op games as much as he did making them, sometimes with too much enthusiasm. (One time, Georges kicked Jarvis out of the arcade for banging on a machine too hard.) Jarvis was of the firm belief that you could tell how well a game was going to perform on wide release based on its first night on test, sometimes even its first hour. A game's earliest moments alive in the dark offered a crucial window into how the game would be received on wide release. If a game's cash box could fill up here, it was bound to fill up elsewhere, too.

Daylight slipping away, the Midway crew left their office at 3401 North California Avenue and headed to Dennis' Place. Their arrival produced zero fanfare. No one really cared or understood who made arcade games. Customers were only interested in the games themselves, and they were eager to try *NBA Jam*.

As an audience gathered around the machine, Sal DiVita popped open the back of the cabinet. Just starting his career in video games, DiVita had become the team's jack-of-all-trades, willing to do almost any task asked of him. In this case, he was responsible for connecting the EPROM into the machine's sockets. DiVita fit the pins in carefully, making a little show of the installation. Then, he closed up and flipped a switch. Electricity flowed. The letters on the marquee brightened to life. The speakers awoke with a pop. The picture came into focus.

Before anyone could step up and claim the first turn, DiVita stood close to the machine so *NBA Jam* could enter attract mode. An arcade game's attract mode consisted of gameplay demos, scoreboards, character bios, logo screens, and other tidbits. When no one was paying to play, the attract mode became bait to hook the next passerby. Letting the attract mode play out would mean that everyone at Dennis' Place would get the first glimpse of *NBA Jam* at the same time.

On the screen, an arena appeared, packed to the rafters with energetic fans. Two teams of two stood on either side of the hardwood, anxious for action. Each player looked remarkably realistic. Out of nowhere, a voice piped up: "Here's the tip!"

At center court, a referee blew his whistle and chucked a ball skyward. When the two players at the middle jumped to grab it, each leapt half his height. A flurry of movement followed: running, passing, stealing, blocking, shoving, shooting. Their jerseys had the eye-popping colors of soda cans.

While *Jam* lifted its slick presentation from broadcast television—at a glance, it could pass for a real NBA game—its play tapped into athletic fantasy. Shoving the other player wasn't just allowed but seemingly an integral part of the game. Fouls were close to nonexistent. The players traded bucket after bucket at a frenetic clip. With a tap of the Turbo button, you moved even faster, temporarily turning your sneakers a bright color.

And then there were the slam dunks. Players hurtled themselves toward the heavens, jumping feet above the rim without a second thought. In midair, they pulled off all manner of cannonballs, spins, and contortions. When they landed at the hoop, the impact was seismic. No one had ever seen a basketball game like this.

Suddenly, the on-court action disappeared. In its place arrived a high score screen announcing the cabinet's "Greatest Players." Since this machine didn't have a scratch on it, *Jam* listed eight sets of initials by default. Seven of the eight lines represented a team member behind the game: "SL" for Shawn Liptak, "RJR" for Jamie Rivett, "SAL" for Sal DiVita, "TWG" for Tony Goskie, and so on. (Midway artist Tim Coman grabbed the last spot as "TJC.")

Game developers usually labored under a shroud of anonymity, but at Midway, things were different. Employees snuck their names, faces, and voices into their games wherever they could. They loved coming up with in-jokes and secrets, toying with the truth, and taking liberties if it meant making a better game. When it came to video games at Midway, reality was considered boring. No one was going to pay for reality. Instead, the magic was in "exaggerated reality," where games looked like real life but played like something else.

The *NBA Jam* team had pored over the game, working 80 hours a week to get it ready for its debut. Everything from the player heads, hand-drawn by Tony Goskie, to the propulsive music, written by Jon

Hey, was top of the line. The seven of them relentlessly argued over how the game should look and play, but they shared a deep creative camaraderie. They had already begun to celebrate the absurd world they had built by gambling their own cash on rounds of *NBA Jam*. When the last buzzer sounded on a heated match, chairs and four-letter words were liable to fly.

Shimmering atop the Greatest Players scoreboard were the initials "MJT," which stood for Mark Joseph Turmell. Six-foot-five and lanky, with long Robert Plant hair and a passion for mischief and compulsive fun, the 29-year-old Turmell was the mastermind behind *NBA Jam*. He was at a new point in his career: After experiencing incredible success designing games across a variety of platforms for over a decade, Turmell's second coin-op at Midway, *Total Carnage*, was a commercial flop. Getting his third arcade game to test had not been without its hurdles—at one point, the NBA stood firm about not granting Midway its license—but Turmell was certain he was onto something huge here.

The attract mode then ran a second roll call, this one filled with figures that the crowd would recognize. The names and faces of the NBA's hottest stars and rising prospects flew by: Charles Barkley, Shawn Kemp, Hakeem Olajuwon, Scottie Pippen, Isiah Thomas, Patrick Ewing, Shaquille O'Neal, Glen Rice, and loads more. In total, the game had 56 players. This, too, was a revelation. No basketball video game had ever offered so many playable NBA stars whose faces you could recognize in the menus and on the court itself.

If there was ever a time to set a basketball game loose in the Windy City, this was it. Led by Michael Jordan, the biggest name in the sport and fast becoming one of the most famous people on Earth, the Chicago Bulls were back-to-back NBA champions with a third trophy in their sights. Over the summer, Jordan and the best players in the league had met up in Barcelona for the 1992 Summer Olympics. The Dream Team, as they were called, cruised to gold medals. The air was thick with the fever of victory.

A customer approached *NBA Jam* and fed the machine its first token. Dennis Georges's military portrait disappeared into the slot, and the customer pressed the start button. The Midway guys moved away and settled in at tables nearby to watch the activity from a distance. Turmell and DiVita cracked open their notebooks. Turmell, in particular, loved observing how people played his games. Big, loud reactions were his creative fuel.

Patron after patron sank token after token into the machine, acclimating to the rules and rhythms of its unfamiliar world. The game's high-energy commentary provided by Tim Kitzrow instantly stood out. Along with calling the on-court action factually as it happened, Kitzrow had a seemingly limitless repertoire of quips and phrases for every scenario: "From downtown!" for a big three; "*Re*-jected!" for a huge block; "The nail in the coffin!" for a bucket that sealed their opponents' fate; "Jams it in!" for an emphatic dunk. Kitzrow's tongue-in-cheek delivery ensured every exchange would be entertaining, and players quickly took to imitating his inflections. Even amidst the racket on the arcade floor, his voice carried.

"He's heating up!"

"HE'S ON FIRE!"

"BOOMSHAKALAKA!"

By 11 p.m., it was a clear that the customers of Dennis' Place for Games loved *NBA Jam*. The Midway gang celebrated the occasion by leaving to get slices of New York-style pizza, then headed back before close to get more feedback. At 2 a.m., as the machine was powered down and crowds poured out of the arcade into the streets of Chicago, the team was riding high.

Still, their work wasn't done. On the game's second and third nights on test, Turmell and DiVita returned to Dennis' Place. *NBA Jam* continued to perform exceptionally well, but they began to notice issues.

For example, the presence of familiar NBA players led players to assume that their avatars had been programmed to have the same skills as their real-life equivalents. "Don't even put it on the floor next to Stockton," one customer told another, referencing the light-fingered point guard on the Utah Jazz. "He'll take it every time." Taking advantage of Utah's small man/big man combo of John Stockton and Karl Malone seemed like a sound strategy. The problem was, as *NBA*

Jam artist John Carlton pointed out, the code never accounted for any variety in player attributes. The players were like M&M's: No matter how different they appeared on the outside, they were all the same on the inside. Turmell and DiVita took note.

Another interaction was harder to watch. One kid stepped up, coined in, and tapped Start on Player 2's panel but used Player 3's controls. As the other players zigzagged after the ball, Player 2 stood off to a side, staring into space. With the wrong joystick and buttons in his hands, every movement the kid made was meaningless. Somehow, he was oblivious to what was happening.

As a rule, Turmell didn't interfere with a game on test, but this instance necessitated a conversation, so he got up and introduced himself. "You're on Player 3," Turmell said, gesturing to the controls. "You're actually on Player 2." Embarrassed by the mistake, the kid thanked him and moved to the correct panel. Turmell returned to DiVita and they both shuddered at the awkward user experience. "What a disaster," one said to the other.

Yet barely a minute later, the kid was back on Player 3, doing nothing and loving it. Maybe the problem was with him, maybe it was with how the game explained its controls. Either way, this apparent foolishness was too much to ignore, so the *Jam* team added prominent color-coded windows that identified which paying player was which before tip-off. A menu on the back end would allow arcade operators to turn "idiot boxes" on or off.

Hour after hour, day after day, crowds would continue to huddle around *NBA Jam*—not just the machine at Dennis' Place, but the thousands that shipped across the country and beyond. Over the next year, the team would witness their baby become a phenomenon. *Jurassic Park* would become the biggest movie of 1993, accumulating $346 million within a year of release. In that same timeframe, *NBA Jam* would *triple* that number, pulling in over $1 *billion*—one quarter at a time.

Players across the globe would perfect *NBA Jam* techniques and dig for secrets. Magazines would splash the game across their covers. The game would come to be adored by the press, the public, other game developers, and even the very NBA superstars depicted in its pixels. In the hands of Acclaim Entertainment, *NBA Jam* would blow up all over again in the home market. Advertisements would appear in magazines and comic books, and commercials on television sets and movie theater screens. A sprawling cast of hidden characters would be buried within its games: politicians, musicians, actors, baseball players, football players, and armies of programmers. *NBA Jam* would let you ball as the Prince of Wales or the Fresh Prince of Bel-Air.

There would be updates, sequels, spin-offs, remakes, and rip-offs. Midway would launch an entire arcade sports division on *NBA Jam*'s back. The game would even lead to bitter heartbreak for its creators who watched it first soar on West Belmont Avenue. In time, the team would witness not just the fall of the *NBA Jam* name but the arcade game industry and finally the Williams Bally/Midway empire itself.

But as those opening nights on test wound down, *NBA Jam* was far from conquering the world. It was still a game with a broken feature that needed to be fixed.

After mulling over what to do about Stockton and Malone, Turmell and DiVita left Dennis' Place for Games before close one night and circled back to the office. Cutting past the rows of half-finished pinball tables and arcade cabinets that filled the factory floor, they made it to the developers' area at the back of the building and switched on their computers. Under each player's portrait on the team select screen, DiVita began adding tiny text and bars representing the key attributes that differentiated them: "Speed," "3 Ptrs," "Dunks," and "Def." For the Utah Jazz, he turned John Stockton lightning fast and cranked up Karl Malone's ability to dunk. Stockton and Malone would be a one-two punch, just like the real thing. There was still much more work for Turmell and DiVita to do, but *NBA Jam*'s potential for strategy immediately deepened.

This was a start. In a few hours, it would be light again. Another full day at Midway lay ahead. They would be back in the arcade soon enough.

CHAPTER 1:
"HERE'S THE TIP"

THE COIN-OPERATED VIDEO GAME business started on top of a wine barrel in a bar in California.

One day in the summer of 1972, Al Alcorn stopped in at Andy Capp's Tavern as he often did. A programmer at the nearby computer company Atari, Inc., Alcorn visited the bar in Sunnyvale as part of a route of businesses with pinball machines that Atari maintained for a fee. In this instance, Alcorn brought along something to leave behind: a 4-foot-tall electronic game with a screen. He set up a sawed-off milk jug inside the machine to catch any falling change. The game was *Pong*, and it ran a quarter a play.

Pong drilled table tennis down to its essence. Two players each controlled a knob that moved a paddle up and down either side of the screen. A dotted net stood between them, and a ball bounced back and forth. If the ball ricocheted off the first player's paddle and slipped past the second player into the expanse, the first player scored a point. During back-and-forth rallies, play accelerated. The *Pong* arcade game was just a series of white lines on a black background, but it was minimalism at its mightiest.

Nolan Bushnell, the co-founder of Atari, had been dreaming of a game like that for years. In the early 1960s, a teenage Bushnell worked at Lagoon, a popular amusement park nestled in the leafy hills of Farmington, Utah. Rising from peddling a "spill the milk" carnival game to managing a section of the park, Bushnell was responsible for overseeing large arcades filled with coin-op novelties, electromechanical contraptions, and pinball tables. For a penny a turn, parkgoers could play cast-iron cranes, bowling, skee-ball, "love tester" games, and other machines. The games at Lagoon were fun, Bushnell thought, but the technology was so unsophisticated and the experience was so underwhelming. He had seen what games could *really* be.

Bushnell was more than just an enterprising young carnie. He was also a student at the University of Utah, where he had witnessed the future in action at a school computer lab. Programmed by Steve Russell, the 1962 space combat game *Spacewar!* featured white spaceships firing at one another in the black chasm of outer space, marking what was possibly the first computer game.

Bushnell understood that if he could find a way to rig a computer with a game like this on it to a coin slot, it was guaranteed to make money at the arcade. The trouble was figuring out how to bring such high-end technology to the mass market without breaking the bank.

The solution, as Bushnell found, would be to chop a full-sized computer down to a motherboard (essentially, a fancy signal generator), and build machines out of cheap and easily reproducible parts. After he graduated university, Bushnell left Utah for California and the budding Silicon Valley to put his idea into motion. He struck up a partnership with an electrical engineer named Ted Dabney, and the two began working with Nutting Associates, a coin-op game manufacturer, on a *Spacewar!*-like space shooter of their own. In 1971, Nutting Associates rolled out *Computer Space* as the first coin-op video game. But with gameplay that was too complex for its own good, *Computer Space* did not take off.

Feeling that Nutting Associates botched *Computer Space*'s release and eager to strike out on their own, Bushnell and Dabney formed Atari, Inc. to release their second game. Shortly after opening the company in Sunnyvale, Atari landed a talented programmer named Al Alcorn with the promise of working on a major contract. General Electric had commissioned Atari to make a home TV ping-pong game. The game needed to incorporate "one ball, two paddles, and a score," and Bushnell wanted Alcorn to be the one to design it. Under Bushnell's direction, Alcorn programmed *Pong*. Atari then built a makeshift arcade cabinet for the game and left it at Andy Capp's Tavern to get a feel for how the public would respond to the concept.

A couple of weeks after leaving *Pong* behind, Alcorn checked in to see how the machine was doing. The owner of Andy Capp's expressed his amazement at its success. When he came to open the bar, he would find customers waiting around outside so they could get back in and get back to *Pong*. As the legend goes, when Alcorn unlocked the door to the game's cash box, quarters came flooding out of the milk jug. This good sign was only the beginning for *Pong*.

In reality, there was no General Electric contract—Bushnell had concocted the whole story to give Alcorn a test assignment before Alcorn tackled Atari's real next project—but Alcorn evidently didn't mind much. The arcade format turned out to be the perfect vessel for *Pong*, too. Its play was fast and thrilling, its rhythmic mechanic easy to understand but difficult to master, and its two-player action added an intriguing social component.

Pong went into wide release on November 29, 1972. The game proved to be a smash across demographics, selling an astounding 19,000 units. Countless *Pong* knock-off machines followed for both arcades and home TV sets. *Pong* wasn't the first video game ever made, but its popularity was so overwhelming that it was often misremembered as such. Sports, not space, would be the rocket to the moon for coin-op games that Nolan Bushnell envisioned at Lagoon.

But as a genre, sports games had a long, long way to go before they reached their potential. After all, *Pong*'s ball wasn't even round—it was square.

In 1974, Midway Manufacturing Company mailed out an important bulletin to arcade operators and distributors. The well-reputed manufacturer of pinball tables and coin-op amusements based out of Schiller Park, Illinois, was putting out another one of its first video games. The colorful flyer for *TV Basketball* boasted a picture of the cabinet, drawings of generic basketball players, and boxes touting such features as two- or four-player games, adjustable time control, and "realistic player images and baskets."

In the game, two pairs of players split a court with basketball nets positioned on either side and a ball bouncing between them. Each duo moved up and down the screen in sync, attempting to score by striking the ball through the net on the opposite side. Truth be told, *TV Basketball* was just another glorified *Pong* clone, but at the time, this was as high-quality as two-on-two arcade basketball was going to get. Though the four players were faceless sprites, *TV Basketball* likely marked the first time a video game featured humans as playable characters.

Midway took a shot on *TV Basketball* by importing it from Taito, a Japanese game company, for the American market. The move paid off, with the game selling an enormous 1,400 cabinets. *TV Basketball* was the first hoops game in the arcade, hot on the heels of

1973's *Basketball* for the Magnavox Odyssey, itself the first home game console. In order to play *Basketball* on the Odyssey, you had to lay a sheet of translucent plastic on your television screen. The overlay featured illustrations of ten stick figures scattered around a court. Controllers in hand, you played a *Pong*-esque ball-and-paddle game, and kept score by hand on pen and paper. Pretending the experience simulated actual basketball required heaps of imagination.

Early sports games had the blandest and most straightforward titles: *Tennis*, *Golf*, *Baseball*. Owing to this, other games called *Basketball* also surfaced, each simple and unlicensed. None were connected to the National Basketball Association, the increasingly popular pro league, until Mattel released *NBA Basketball* for the Intellivision in 1980. You couldn't play as any actual teams or players in *NBA Basketball*, but the mere act of having the logo on the box signaled a major development for fans who wanted to experience NBA action in a new way. The league found a potentially lucrative licensing avenue, too.

Trip Hawkins, CEO of Electronic Arts, took this notion to the next logical step in 1982. As a huge fan of the San Francisco 49ers, Hawkins had the idea of creating a game based on Joe Montana that put you in the cleats of the star quarterback and Super Bowl MVP. Professional athletes had never been in a video or computer game before, but making a game with Montana's likeness was good as money in the bank. But as Hawkins pressed further, he found that Montana had already signed a deal with Atari to endorse its product line.

Undeterred, Hawkins pivoted from football and applied the same concept to a basketball game. He struck a deal with "Dr. J" Julius Erving, his favorite player. The Philadelphia 76ers icon flew to EA's studio in California for principal photography, and Hawkins quickly realized he needed a second huge name to make the game really pop. For $25,000 and a 2.5 percent royalty rate per likeness, Hawkins put the pieces in motion for *One on One: Dr. J vs. Larry Bird*.

On the court, Erving and Bird were NBA mega-stars and ferocious rivals. Their pixelated counterparts were simple but effective simulations, and *One on One* allowed you to play as either. Keenly aware of the technological deficiencies of the popular Atari 2600 console, Hawkins planned *One on One* as a computer game for the Apple II. Working with a state-of-the-art home computer and making the game mano-a-mano instead of five-on-five allowed Hawkins to take full advantage of the available processing power.

One on One was coded by Eric Hammond, a 19-year-old programmer who met with Erving and Bird to capture footage, soak up inspiration, and pepper them with questions about basketball. To make the game's graphics, Hammond used a crude motion-capture process where he filmed Dr. J dunking and carefully animated each frame so his in-game avatar moved with the same authentic quality, albeit at a molasses-slow five frames per second. Hammond enlivened *One on One* with cool details—an in-game scoreboard, a 24-second shot clock, the steady ticking sound of a dribbling ball, the whoosh of a cheering crowd—and built a fun little game. If you leaped up and slammed hard enough, you could shatter the glass backboard, at which point a janitor would appear to sweep up the shards and grumble over the mess you made.

Released in 1983, *One on One: Dr. J vs. Larry Bird* reveled in its star power and realism. "We put the two of them together on a dream court of light, for an electronic afternoon of one-on-one," read one ad. *One on One* was a critical and financial success, with the magazine *St. Game* describing it as "a game that feels like the real thing." In its wake, Electronic Arts made a sequel called *Jordan vs. Bird: One on One* and soon established EA Sports, a division dedicated solely to sports games.

As developers experimented with new ways to bring basketball to screens, innovations trickled along. Konami's 1986 arcade title *Double Dribble* featured colorful graphics, five-on-five action, cutaway animations for dunks, and a tinny version of "The Star-Spangled Banner" before tip-off, but its players had little personality and its commentary sounded robotic. *Magic Johnson's Fast Break*, Arcadia Systems's 1988 two-on-two coin-op game, had good graphics, detailed characters, and audio clips of Johnson's voice, but its gameplay was awkwardly fast and unremarkable.

By the late 80s, a basketball game seemingly couldn't go out the door without having a license. NBA stars scored starring roles in console titles like *Bill Laimbeer's Combat Basketball* and *David Robinson's Supreme Court*. Even a coach got in on the action with *Pat Riley Basketball*. Following the release of *Jordan Vs. Bird: One on One*, Electronic Arts introduced *Lakers versus Celtics and the NBA Playoffs*, a game with increasingly robust simulation aspects. The NBA Playoffs series would evolve into the hit NBA Live franchise.

Still solely known for games on the arcade market, the Midway name hadn't appeared near a hoops title since *TV Basketball*, and the company was long overdue for a follow-up. Midway's next game was also two-on-two. It featured large players with distinct looks, a court, a crowd, cheerleaders, four periods, and the ability to rough up your opponent. It had big dunks and, like *Dr. J vs. Larry Bird*, even let you break the backboard. A giant red and blue logo adorned the sides of its cabinet. The game was a hit in the arcades—but it wasn't *NBA Jam*.

CHAPTER 2:
"FROM DOWNTOWN"

ON THE BOTTOM FLOOR of a hotel in Chicago, Eugene Jarvis could do anything. If he wanted, at that very moment, Jarvis could wipe out aliens from a spaceship, burn rubber in a racecar, or command a tank under heavy enemy fire. Best of all: He could do it all without having to leave the convention carpet. Each flickering fantasy lived in its own cabinet, and the floor of the 1980 Amusement and Music Operators Association (AMOA) expo was packed with them.

By fall 1980, Atari's successes had pushed video games to the forefront of pop culture. Game companies sprouted like weeds across the world. The Atari 2600 console jump-started the lucrative home market, cementing Atari as the premier name in the business. With its vast library of games, the Atari 2600 had made the video games a staple of the American living room.

But the real action was in the arcade. Coin-op games offered juicier graphics, higher grade hardware, and more engaging gameplay than anything available on a console. Innovative machines from companies such as Atari, Namco, and Cinematronics began drawing huge crowds of players across all ages. There was a boom of storefront video arcades, and game rooms opened far and wide. In America, arcades started along main streets in big cities, then fanned out into suburbs and malls until they became a ubiquitous part of youth culture. On its own, an arcade cabinet could end up anywhere: a bowling alley, a bar, a truck stop, a grocery store. Every game could have its own shape, art, controls, and personality.

Coin-op games drove the entire game industry. They were why arcade operators, executives, businesspeople, and game makers moved through the hallways of the Conrad Hilton hotel. AMOA was a hunt for the next great quarter-eater, and the impressive contenders included *Battlezone*, *Berzerk*, *Star Castle*, and *Crazy Climber*.

Jarvis was attending on behalf of his employer, Williams Electronics, Inc. Established in 1943, the Chicago-based Williams was a longstanding manufacturer of pinball tables and novelty amusement games. The company, which went by a variety of names including Williams Manufacturing Company and Williams Electronic Manufacturing Company, had dipped its toes into the game business with a *Pong* clone. The game performed so well that the company realized that video was the future of the coin-op business. At AMOA, Williams was debuting *Defender*, its first original video game. It happened to be Jarvis's first video game, too.

Bright-eyed and brilliant, with a playful smile, a sly sense of humor, and a soft spot for expletives, the 25-year-old Jarvis had a longstanding affair with coin-op games. He grew up in Menlo Park, California, where he would sneak over to Johnny's Smoke Shop, a convenience store with candy and adult magazines in the front, and gambling tables and pinball machines in the back. Jarvis relished how coin-devouring quick-reflex games tapped into his "reptilian brain," his description for the section of the brain that craved immediate stimulation. If anything could tickle those tendencies, it would be *Defender*.

Co-created by Jarvis and Larry DeMar, *Defender* was a space shooter with roots dating back to Steve Russell's *Spacewar!*, like so many games at the time. But unlike other shooters with confined screens and limited color palettes, *Defender* felt wide open and used a rainbow of color. Instead of being limited to shooting enemies on a single vertical field, you flew your ship up and down across interconnected horizontal screens. The side-scrolling element added a clever twist on the genre.

The game wasn't just innovative. It was also lightning-fast and mercilessly tough. If you weren't paying attention, you were finished as soon as you started. As a result, no one at AMOA was sticking around on *Defender* for very long. Jarvis noticed the lack of interest, but he wasn't too concerned. For him, the convention wasn't so much about promoting his game as it was doing what he called "market research" (that is, playing other video games).

Crossing the carpet, Jarvis wandered over to see what was going on at Midway's booth. Located in the nearby Franklin Park, Midway Manufacturing Company was Williams's local rival, and a phenomenally successful one at that. Midway's strategy of Westernizing Japanese video games like *TV Basketball* had paid off in a massive way. In 1978, the company licensed a space shooter from Taito called *Space Invaders*, creating a cultural frenzy even bigger than *Pong*. At AMOA, Midway was showing off Namco-made games it had brought over to America, including *Rally-X* and *Pac-Man*.

Jarvis joined the long line of people waiting to try *Pac-Man*. When he saw the game in action, he had trouble wrapping his head around how this was going to be successful. While its mechanic was novel, how the hell was it going to make any money? If you played *Defender*, you could be toast in seconds. An ordinary round of *Pac-Man* lasted entire minutes.

Time was money in coin-op games, Jarvis had learned, and he was eager to absorb every trick and lesson he could to make the most successful games possible. Aside from being a top-notch programmer, Jarvis had a knack for coming up with good ideas and articulating concepts in interesting ways. In a TV interview, he described video games as "participatory cinema" and "a way in which you can react and have feedback and exist within the reality of the TV set."

By the time AMOA wrapped up, the attendees' consensus was that neither *Defender* nor *Pac-Man* was the star of the show. Instead, all the businesspeople showered praise on Midway's racing game *Rally-X*.

But over the following year, the industry experts would be proven wrong in a major way. *Defender* would sell an incredible 60,000 cabinets and generate over a billion dollars in the arcade, establishing Williams as a major player in video. Midway, on the other hand, would sell a record-setting 400,000 *Pac-Man* cabinets and create a pop culture sensation. The crosstown rivalry between Williams and Midway was heating up.

•

Detroit made cars. Pittsburgh made steel. Chicago made, among other things, coin-op games. The Windy City had been pumping out machines for decades. Chicago had it all: steel from Pennsylvania, lumber from Wisconsin, convenient transportation routes along the Great Lakes, and a bevy of innovative designers in town.

D. Gottlieb & Co's *Baffle Ball* in 1931 and Bally Manufacturing Corporation's *Ballyhoo* in 1932 were the very first coin-op pinball games, and both were made in Chicago. Bally grew into a massive company with interests in several industries, including casinos and gyms. In 1969, Bally acquired Midway Manufacturing Corporation, itself a company that had been producing pinball, puck bowling, and electro-mechanical games for over a decade. In addition to keeping the Midway name active, Bally created a division called Bally Midway.

Considering the city's importance to coin-op games, Eugene Jarvis's ending up in Chicago was inevitable. He started out working on pinball games at Atari on the West Coast, then made the move when Williams offered him a job in its pinball division. When Jarvis arrived at 3401 North California Avenue in 1979, the Williams factory was the liveliest of places. Women chatted as they built pinball machines, the air filled with the smells of cigarette smoke and soldered metal. During World War II, the American government had used the facility to make weapons, and the green paint it added to the walls was still left behind. Williams's neighborhood was on the rundown side, and the building's rat problem was getting worse, but still, this was the place to be.

As the smash success of *Defender* pushed Williams's business way up, Jarvis began having difficulties with the company. Jarvis and Larry DeMar decided to leave Williams to form Vid Kidz, a short-lived independent studio that created games that Williams would then publish and manufacture. First, Vid Kidz produced a sequel to *Defender* called *Stargate*. Then, it made *Robotron: 2084*.

In a futuristic dystopia, an evil line of robots called Robotrons have taken over Earth and nearly exterminated the human race. Armed with a blaster, your job was to protect the last human family by killing every last Robotron. You were dropped into rooms where waves of relentless Robotrons closed in from all angles. The only way to stay alive was to shoot and run, shoot and run, shoot and run. While *Defender* championed freedom of movement, *Robotron* was about confinement.

Unlike other coin-op games, playing *Robotron* did not require the use of buttons. Instead, you used two joysticks: one to control your direction of fire, the other to control your movement. At first, *Robotron* was difficult and felt unfamiliar, but it quickly grew rewarding and compulsively playable.

Released in 1982, *Robotron: 2084* was one of a fleet of simple but addictive games responsible that pushed the arcade business to its highest height. Thousands of arcades were open across America. Reports estimated that coin-op games generated $200 to $300 billion worldwide in 1982. That year, Williams and Midway each did around $200 million in revenue. Each company was rolling out classics: Williams made *Joust*, *Moon Patrol*, and *Sinistar* while Midway was known for *Galaga*, *Spy Hunter*, *Tapper*, *Gorf*, *Satan's Hollow*, and *Tron*.

But just as dramatically as the game industry's fortunes soared, they came screaming back to Earth.

The trouble started with Atari and its lax attitude on product quality. By 1983, the lack of standards for publishing a game on the Atari 2600 meant that anyone who wanted to cash in on the video game craze could enter the market. As a result, the shelves were saturated with subpar games. Meanwhile, Atari's competitors pumped out their own consoles and more mediocre games.

In response, the public got sick of video games as a whole. Supply exceeded demand by unsustainable margins, and the industry crashed. Game industry revenues fell from $3.2 billion in 1983 to $100 million by 1985—a drop of almost 97 percent.

Arcade cabinet sales plummeted, too. Compared to the 60,000 units sold of *Defender* and 19,000 of *Robotron: 2084*, Eugene Jarvis and Larry DeMar's 1983 game *Blaster* sold a paltry 500 cabinets. The video game business looked like it was finished—another fad on the scrap heap of history.

Williams was seriously injured by its failing video game sales and started looking at other technology like payphones. Layoffs came, and the company changed. When it seemed clear that video games were finished, Jarvis returned to California and attended Stanford University to get his master's in business.

Williams and Bally Midway pivoted from video games back to pinball. Both companies released first-rate pinball tables, but the sales just weren't at the same level as video games. This made the success of every release critical, and the rivalry between the two over the market intensified. The businesses were civil but not chummy, and rumors of corporate spying floated around. Williams and Midway were, in Jarvis's words, "eating each other's lunch."

In 1985, Nintendo released the smash-hit Nintendo Entertainment System and set the home game business back on course. As Nintendo created a new game empire, a competitor called Sega soon nipped at its heels. Both companies enforced stringent quality standards and released high-quality games to ensure the Video Game Crash of 1983 wouldn't repeat itself. Atari began to drift off the map.

In California, Eugene Jarvis couldn't stop thinking about games. He still wanted to make more. After graduating from Stanford in the late 1980s, he returned to Chicago to rejoin Williams. While the American home market was roaring, the coin-op business was still on the mend. Williams's video output had slowed to a standstill. Between 1985 and 1987, the company released just one game, *Joust 2*, which sold only a thousand cabinets.

Jarvis couldn't help but compare American arcade games to their Japanese counterparts. In Japan, small armies of skilled artists were making games rich with large character sprites and beautiful stylized worlds. By comparison, Williams's graphics were woefully outdated, but the company couldn't afford the talent and manpower it needed to compete. If Williams was going to stand out in the marketplace, it had to come up with something equally eye-catching and cost-effective. It needed to get creative.

The solution, Jarvis and the team at Williams soon discovered, was called "digitization." Most movies were live action, not animated. Instead of trying to top hand-drawn visuals, why not figure out a way to make realistic-looking games?

In a carefully lit studio, an actor would simulate all of a character's motions—say, walking, jumping, falling, or shooting—against a blue screen. By videotaping the actors, converting the tape to computer graphics, and extracting the actors from their backgrounds, Williams could digitize real people into heroes and villains, then place them into two-dimensional worlds. Midway attempted similar technology in 1983 for a game about the rock band Journey, but that game's low-resolution black-and-white headshots did not come close to the ambitious vision Williams had in mind.

Developers Jarvis, Warren Davis, Todd Allen, and Mark Loffredo worked together to sort out digitization. Figuring how to make this concept feasible was a difficult and time-consuming process, but the team was up to the task, designing their own hardware. Even in the aftermath of the Video Game Crash, the company was stacked with sharp and hungry talent, including programmer George Petro and artist Jack Haeger. The game everyone was working on was called *Narc*.

You played as Max Force or Hit Man, two motorcycle-helmet-wearing vigilantes hellbent on cleaning up the streets of a twisted take on Chicago. Your job was to wipe out drug dealers and users with guns, flamethrowers, and rocket launchers, spraying body parts and creating chaos on the streets. Venturing through subways and hideouts, you dodged bullets, needles, attack dogs, and evil clowns all in an effort to reach Mr. Big, a seedy *Scarface*-style drug kingpin who was, in actuality, developer Mark Loffredo. You could arrest certain criminals if you liked, too, but where was the fun in that? Released in 1988, *Narc* was gritty, absurd, indulgent, and eerily realistic. In other words, it was nothing anyone had ever seen from Williams before. Arcade operators balked at the game's violence and subject matter, but any controversy was quickly forgotten when crowds swarmed the game. The company sold over 3,000 cabinets, solidifying *Narc* as a real hit. Just like that, Williams was a contender in the game business again.

Thousands of feet above Earth, floating through the clouds toward Reno, Jeff Nauman was struck with a sudden urge: He needed a barf bag. Nauman wasn't sick, but he did need to get something out. He retrieved a bag, then a flight attendant brought him a pen, so he began to make notes. He had an idea for his next project at Bally Midway. It would be basketball, and it would be two-on-two. You would trade control of the ball between you and a computer-controlled teammate, and you would be able to move around the court and execute real plays. The game he came up with would be called *Arch Rivals*.

When Nauman touched ground again, he excitedly shared his idea with Brian Colin, his friend and creative accomplice. The inseparable duo of Nauman and Colin were two of Bally Midway's most prolific and effective designers. As programmer and artist, Nauman and Colin made games as varied as *Xenophobe*, a *Star Trek*-inspired sidescroller; *Demolition Derby*, a chaotic car game; and *Rampage*, a chomp-'em, stomp-'em game where movie monsters punched skyscrapers and wrecked a helpless city.

Nauman and Colin began working together in the early 1980s when Bally Midway was recruiting talent to develop original games in Franklin Park, a village outside Chicago. The offices were small and cramped, but the work was hands-on and everybody was friendly. Paired with a lot of creative freedom and little managerial oversight, Bally Midway was a terrific place to work, even through the Video Game Crash.

To make *Arch Rivals* happen, Nauman had to convince Colin that they could make a basketball game that would appeal to arcadegoers who were not basketball fans. If Colin was going to sign on, the game needed something to keep him interested. The hook, they found, was putting in the punching mechanic from *Rampage*. Like the creatures in that game, *Arch Rivals* players could throw haymakers—only now they were doing it right on the court.

The game would have no license, but that wasn't a problem. Nauman and Colin always liked doing their own thing without having to go through any bureaucratic red tape; the most this game had in common with the NBA was blue and red cabinet sideart that riffed on the league's logo. Instead of real teams and real athletes, the pair created their own teams and developed quirky characters like Tyrone, Hammer, and Mohawk. Each character came with a different description (Tyrone, for example, was a "defensive giant"), but all of them ultimately played the same.

On an isometric plane, players raced around the basketball court, blocking, passing, shooting, and punching. Even with the punching, *Arch Rivals* kept it light and silly, and felt like good, clean fun. Details gave the game life. You could slip on banana peels and candy wrappers chucked onto the court by unruly fans. Heated coaches hovered on the sidelines, one bad play away from losing it. A nearsighted referee wore chunky bifocals. With the court's half-empty bleachers, the setting resembled a varsity scrimmage more than a pro game.

Deep into the game's development, Bally Manufacturing made a dramatic decision. Long removed since the fortunes of *Pac-Man*, years of bad investments caught up to the company. In 1988—the same year *Narc* came out—Bally decided to sell Midway and all its Bally Midway trademarks to none other than Williams Electronics. Williams let go of all of the Bally Midway designers, except for Nauman and Colin. Disheartened by the news but still focused on their game, the pair stayed the course on *Arch Rivals*.

Much to the chagrin of its developers, Williams was going through change, too. A variety of names already represented the company (among others, Williams Electronics Games and WMS Industries, Inc.), and now another one was coming. Williams Electronics would become Williams Bally/Midway. This meant that Williams would not only keep the Midway name alive, but it would rebrand its video game division to Midway.

Eugene Jarvis didn't get it—they had just won a war and here they were about to fly the loser's flag—but Lou Nicastro had made up his mind. "Goddammit, we paid $7 million for that fucking company," Nicastro said. "We're going to use their goddamn name!"

In 1989, *Arch Rivals* rolled out as the first product of the Williams Bally/Midway era. Its flyer's tagline of "Lean, mean profit machine!" proved to be prophetic. Rumor had it that *Arch Rivals* performed so well that it alone covered Williams's purchase of Midway. Acclaim Entertainment, Williams's new partner on the home publishing front, quickly converted the game to consoles and even secured a spot for *Arch Rivals* star Tyrone in *The Power Team*, a cartoon starring video game characters that also featured Max Force from *Narc*.

Arch Rivals performed so well that Neil Nicastro, Lou's son who was taking an increasingly larger role in the company, asked Nauman and Colin to consider remaking the game with four control panels instead of two. More coin slots would mean more money. Jarvis also encouraged them to consider the idea, but Nauman and Colin were not interested. They weren't about to make the same game all over again. Bouncing between genres was as much part of their creative alchemy as the games themselves.

Nauman and Colin weren't fitting in well at Williams either. Williams's work atmosphere had a sense of competitiveness that they didn't like, and as outsiders from a former rival, they felt the cold shoulder. Their lighthearted art style also didn't gel with the realistic visual direction Williams was headed in. The pair often worked out of their homes, and after developing a couple of other games, Nauman and Colin left Williams Bally/Midway in 1992 to establish their own studio, Game Refuge.

Clearly, there was still untapped potential in coin-op basketball. Williams Bally/Midway's next basketball game would come from a recent hire—a talented twenty-something who pulled up to 3401 North California Avenue in a fly yellow Corvette, ready at last to make arcade games of his own.

CHAPTER 3:
"MAGIC CARPET RIDE"

WHEN NIGHT FELL ON BAY CITY, the boys brought out their matches. There were two of them: Mark, a shy, skinny kid with auburn hair and inquisitive blue eyes, and Elmer, his cool and athletic friend. Both were about thirteen.

In 1976, Bay City, Michigan was a town of 30,000 that personified Midwestern suburbia, down to the lofty trees that lined its roads. In the evening, the streets of the suburbs would go quiet, allowing the best friends a chance to hang around and hunt for a new form of entertainment. At the time, their object of fascination was fire.

Out one autumn evening, Mark and Elmer had a really good idea. They found a pile of leaves clogging up a gutter on the side of the road. It was the perfect material for burning. But before they did anything, they laid down some ground rules. In this case, they decided that they would light the flame, drop it onto the pile of leaves, turn around, and walk to the two nearest mailboxes without looking back once. It was only when they reached the second mailbox that they could turn to see what they had done. Part of the fun was imagining and anticipating what was happening behind them.

The boys struck a match or two and dropped them onto the leaves. Then, they turned their backs and started asking questions. Were there just a few leaves burning or something big enough to get them caught? Was there any fire at all?

Once they finally reached the second mailbox, they spun around. In front of them was a healthy blaze, steady and rising. Mark and Elmer sprinted back and stomped out the flames. They then went on their way, the distraction having entertained them for a few minutes. It wasn't enough for Mark and Elmer to just set something on fire. They had to make a game out of it.

When they weren't playing with fire, Mark and Elmer were out shooting hoops, or playing Yahtzee and poker for cash—an unusual hobby for middle-schoolers that the two enjoyed greatly. They climbed up trees by the train tracks and threw rocks at the passing locomotives, and tinkered with sparkler rockets and gunpowder. Other times, the boys hopped on their bikes and headed for the bowling alley where they spent hours feeding coins into games like *Pong*, *Sea Wolf*, and *Breakout*. Mark, in particular, developed a special affinity for video games.

Mark Joseph Turmell was born March 22, 1963 to Joseph, a middle manager at Chevrolet, and Joan, a caring stay-at-home mother. Mark's family also included an older sister, Nancy. Not every family was receptive to video games, but luckily for Mark, his was.

For Christmas 1973, Mark asked for *Pong* or an 8-track stereo. His parents went with the former, picking up a *Pong* console at Sears for $99.99. Mark was overjoyed with his gift, preserving both the machine and the box it came in. He played the game enough to figure out a neat trick. If he interrupted the power flow from the RF modulator to the console just right, he could warp the ball and send it right past his opponent. He was fascinated that the secret existed.

Around the same time he was hanging out with Elmer, Turmell got his first crack at playing with a computer. A friend of his had a newfangled computer terminal borrowed from the nearby Delta College sitting in his home. His dad, a professor at Delta, had brought home a computer, a modem, and a teletype computer terminal with built-in printer. Once hooked to a phone line, the computer could connect to a mainframe computer at Delta, meaning that Turmell and his friend could play text-based games such as *Colossal Cave Adventure*, which set the scene in words alone. His friend had a football game, too, which offered simple prompts like:

```
First And 10 At The 40-Yard Line
******************************
Press 1 for Long Bomb
Press 2 to Sweep Right
```

Once a button was pressed, the game processed an outcome for the scenario and gave you the results on printer paper. Then, it moved onto the next play.

Keyboard in hand, Turmell experimented with the game's menus. Poking behind the interface, he glimpsed the commands that powered the game. Just as with the burning leaves, he wondered how he might make his fun more entertaining. Computers offered something home consoles didn't: the ability to write and edit your own code. What if he didn't just play games but actually made his own?

Turmell grew deeply interested in making games, absorbing whatever books and research material he could find. By fifteen, he was splitting his days attending Western High School in the morning and Delta College in the evening, which allowed him to learn the mysterious (and potentially lucrative) discipline of computer programming. A dedicated student, Turmell quickly picked up BASIC, his first computer language. He began to spend more time researching and writing computer programs at the campus computer lab than he was at high school.

Navigating college was stressful. Turmell was already the shy type, and the age difference only made things more awkward. Checking out books from Delta's library required a driver's license—something Turmell was too young to have. But the people around him at Delta saw his talent and encouraged his development. Turmell even scored a job at the school as a system programmer after he broke into its network and tapped into student files and payroll data; he just wanted to see if he could do it.

By the end of the 1970s, home computers were still prohibitively expensive for the average family, but Turmell knew he needed to have one of his own if he was going to write his own games. First, he got a Bally Astrocade—Bally Manufacturing's home console that allowed users to code games—but the Astrocade turned out to be a flash in the pan.

What he really needed, Turmell decided, was an Apple II. Boasting 16K of memory, an 8-bit 6502 microprocessor, and an operating system built on BASIC, it was state-of-the-art technology. Turmell asked his parents to loan him $1,400 to get the computer, and they agreed under the condition that he pay them back by mowing lawns.

As a child, the basement had made Turmell uneasy, but once it became the home for his new Apple II, he practically lived down there. With unlimited access to his own computer, he went into tunnel vision. Long teenage nights melted away as he wrote and revised and re-revised code for long stretches at a time. Ten months after he followed the Apple II into the basement, Turmell walked back upstairs with his first game.

Sneakers was a space shooter in which you moved a spaceship horizontally across the bottom of the screen, wiping out fields of enemies in gameplay similar to Bally Midway's *Gorf.* Your opponents were the Sneakers, kooky brightly colored creatures who darted around in tennis shoes. Like nearly every other programmer in those days, Turmell did everything in *Sneakers* on his own: the design, the code, the graphics, the sound. Even with the technological limitations the Apple II ultimately presented, he worked on *Sneakers* obsessively until it was as playable as an arcade game.

Leafing through a computer magazine, Turmell found a phone number for Sirius Software. Headquartered in Sacramento, California, Sirius was just the kind of thriving company in the early 80s video game boom that might roll the dice on his product, especially considering he used Sirius's own E-Z Draw software to design the game's graphics. Turmell gave the company a call, then sent them a package. Sirius was so impressed by what they received that after a few more phone calls, they were flying him to California to sign a deal.

Sirius released *Sneakers* for the Apple II in July 1981. Within a couple of months, orders were placed for half of the game's 20,000-copy production run. Turmell went from mowing lawns at $7 an hour to making games for $10,000 in monthly royalty checks. His parents promptly directed his earnings toward mutual funds; paying them back for the Apple II got lost in the shuffle. Turmell, meanwhile, was thinking bigger, and planned to upgrade his ordinary Chevrolet Citation to a better ride soon.

Turmell was not alone in his unexpected success. He was one of a handful of "vidkids"—fresh-faced computer programmers who were using the perplexing new tools of computers and video games to get rich. A writer from the computer magazine *Softline* visited Bay City to profile Turmell for its November 1981 issue. The story portrayed him as an enterprising but timid talent who kept himself entertained with his work. "The only problem with having someone like Mark in class," Delta professor Marjorie Leeson told *Softline*, "is that they never want to go home."

The seclusion and concentration Turmell required to make his games did take their toll. Growing up, he enjoyed playing sports, and at eighteen, he was an imposing 6'4" and made an ideal candidate for the Western High School basketball team. But the conflicting obligations of programming courses at Delta and basketball practice at Western meant that he had to decide between the two. He picked the courses.

Turmell's social life also suffered. Throughout high school, he never had a girlfriend nor so much as went to a dance. The very thought of holding a girl's hand made his palms sweat profusely. He had even grown distant from friends like Elmer. To blow off steam, Turmell headed to the arcade and turned his attention to *Asteroids* and *Frogger*.

Turmell's parents always wanted him to go to law school, but the programming opportunities kept coming. A local engineering firm hired Turmell to debug a sewer management program that calculated flow volumes. He composed an inventory program for a quick-print shop, another that ran payroll, a third to do bidding estimates for a construction company. Turmell was laser-focused on his passion for programming to the point of stubbornness. Once, he got into an argument with his math teacher and spouted off. "I don't need to study algebra," Turmell said, "because I'm going to make millions of dollars inventing video games."

For his follow-up on the Apple II, Turmell made a vertical platformer in the style of *Donkey Kong* in which you played a stick figure who climbed ladders, outran creatures, and caught falling objects. When the game was almost finished, Turmell sent it to Sirius for feedback. Sirius CEO Jerry Jewell was inspired to set up a deal to turn the falling objects into cans of ice-cold beer. Olympia Brewing Company loved the idea, and the project turned into *Beer Run*. Just like that, Turmell had his first licensed game before he was old enough to buy a can of Olympia for himself.

Olympia's TV commercials touted "artesian well water" as the source of their beer's fresh taste. Turmell found a clever way to insert that piece of ad lingo into the game. Up by the score, a line of text occasionally appeared, teasing "Artesians just above." But by the time *Beer Run* shipped, there were no Artesians in the game. Ever the mischief maker, Turmell never intended to actually design the Artesians or explain who they were. He just wanted to stoke players' imaginations and give them something to work toward.

Video games allowed Turmell to not only make substantial sums of money but also put him in touch with fellow rising tech luminaries. In 1981, on the invitation of Steve Wozniak, he flew to California to see the Apple co-founder get married. With rides, a hot air balloon, and popcorn vendors, the wedding was more like a carnival, and its extravagance was unlike anything Turmell had ever seen. He caught up with Wozniak at the reception. After being seriously injured in an aircraft accident, Wozniak had passed his recovery time playing *Sneakers*, and he invited Turmell as a thank you.

At another point that day, an entrepreneur in glasses introduced himself to Turmell and pitched him on his fledgling Washington-based computer company that had just turned six years old. "I like your games," Bill Gates said. "Want to come join Microsoft?" Turmell was flattered by the offer, but he had to pass. The future, he explained to Gates, was in video game cartridges.

Back in Michigan, after graduating from Western High School early and completing his coursework at Delta College, Turmell plotted his next move. He was enrolled at Ferris State University, a Michigan school a couple of hours away from Bay City, but he couldn't shake the allure of big-time video game development and the lifestyle that a move to California would afford him. In Sacramento, Sirius Software was keeping a spot on the team warm for him, plus $40,000 in salary and a generous royalty system.

In 1982, Turmell found himself at a crossroads: Stay comfortable in the Midwest and keep pursuing degrees in computer science and marketing, where he was sure to find a good job, or jump into the unfamiliar world of the video game industry. At just nineteen, Turmell was ready for uncertainty and adventure.

To his relief, he thrived in California. In the thick of the booming computer and video game industry, he was finally among his own kind at Sirius. Turmell started creating game cartridges for the Atari 2600 like *Fast Eddie*, *Gas Hog*, and *Turmoil* (the latter of which was a play on his name).

The consistent quality of Turmell's games fast netted him personal fans. One of his followers was John Romero, a young programmer just a few years behind Turmell in the Apple II homebrew scene. Romero looked at his Apple II computer as his personal home arcade, and Turmell's *Free Fall* was one of his favorite games. While Romero was newer to the Apple II scene, he read about Turmell in an issue of *Creative Computing* and hoped to catch up to his success. He wrote a fan letter to Turmell to learn more about *Beer Run*'s masking and rendering effects, and how he managed to put a Sirius Software blimp on the screen. Turmell wrote back, and the ambitious developers started keeping in touch.

Life in Sacramento was good. Sirius's workplace atmosphere was relaxed and playful. Outside the office, adult interests came into focus for Turmell: women, drugs, dancing, nightclubs, rock concerts. He gained more confidence, began wearing nicer clothes, and started growing his hair out into a long curly mane. California was changing him.

In 1983, *People* magazine caught up with Turmell for a profile on the vidkids. The 1981 *Softline* story portrayed him as a reserved kid who was earnestly dedicated to his code. But in *People*, he had a devil-may-care attitude and strong opinions. Turmell predicted that software houses would soon be promoting their major talents like "rock stars," and bristled at how he was discussed professionally. "I am not a programmer, I'm a video game designer," he insisted. The article was a study in new money extravagance, with Turmell rolling around in a red Porsche 924 Turbo. "I'm not a millionaire," he clarified. "Yet."

Between their days programming Atari 2600 games, Turmell and his friends took trips out to The Game Room, an arcade in an outdoor mall in Sacramento. It was there, in 1982, that he first played his favorite game of all time: *Robotron: 2084*. *Defender* was one of Turmell's favorites, but this latest game from Eugene Jarvis was on another level. Mesmerized by the game, Turmell spent hours dodging attacks and blasting robots. He especially loved those close calls, those moments when it looked like the Robotrons had finally cornered you and there was no way possible way out—until you figured out a solution at the last second. Seeing a great *Robotron* player at work made Turmell proud to be a human being. He was part of the same species that mastered that game.

In 1984, Sirius Software suffered the effects of the Video Game Crash and folded up shop. Turmell quickly found other opportunities in California. He landed at Activision, where he worked on Commodore 64 games such as *Toy Bizarre* and *Fast Tracks*. At Activision, hot-shot programmers like Turmell were superstars. They were such valuable commodities that the company would split Turmell and his colleagues up onto separate planes in case there was ever a crash.

After Activision, Turmell moved to a curious project called NEMO. A collaboration between toy empire Hasbro and Nolan Bushnell's Isix, NEMO integrated VHS and video game technologies to create playable interactive movies. During the filming of a new Police Academy movie, Turmell joined the production to gather footage for a game. But NEMO did not last. It was a pet project of Hasbro CEO Stephen D. Hassenfeld, and when Hassenfeld died due to complications from AIDS, the operation was shut down.

Hungry for more cutting-edge technology, Turmell began thinking of the Midwest. The concept of making arcade games at Williams Electronics in Chicago was enticing. It was a notable company, and he could work alongside Eugene Jarvis. The door had been open for years. In high school, Turmell had been contacted by Ken Fedesna, Williams's Executive Vice President, about working with the company, but nothing materialized.

This time, Turmell decided to do the reaching out. Fedesna was still very interested.

Turmell flew out to Chicago to have dinner with Fedesna and the Williams employees, who were fresh off *Narc* and its breakthrough technology. The Williams gang was a casual T-shirt-and-jeans crew. Meanwhile, the towering Turmell showed up wearing a turquoise jacket and black-and-white wingtip shoes, his long hair extending to his shoulders.

The Williams guys were taken aback by Turmell's flamboyance. *Narc* programmer and Williams veteran George Petro had no clue what to make of him. "Who is this guy?" Petro thought. "He looks like he stepped out of a music video." Turmell gave off the vibe of an "idea guy" more than someone who could get a game out the door. Williams didn't need any idea guys. They had enough of their own.

After dinner, Turmell invited the Williams crew back to his hotel room to show them a game he was really into at the time. He had set up a Macintosh to run *Crystal Quest*, an action game in which your enemies poured in from the sides of the screen. It was a little like *Robotron: 2084*. Turmell was clearly smitten, but the appeal of *Crystal Quest*—and why the Williams guys had to see it—was lost on them.

The next day, the team discouraged Fedesna from making Turmell an offer. Jarvis hadn't attended the dinner, but based on what he heard, he too was skeptical. But Fedesna stood firm about hiring him. Williams management had already anointed him as someone special. Mark Turmell was coming back to the Midwest.

One morning in March 1989, Turmell arrived at the Williams Electronics office to start his first day. He parked a yellow Corvette, its license plate reading "MR-LZUR." George Petro got a look at the plate and struggled to decipher it. Mr. El-zur? Mr. Luh-zur? Mr. Loser? "Mr. Leisure!" Turmell clarified. "Oh," Petro responded. "I don't get it." There was a lot about Turmell that no one at Williams got.

In order to get to his desk every day, Turmell had a long walk past the hundreds of workers assembling pinball and arcade games piece by piece. The developers were clustered at the back of the building. The top floor was dedicated to pinball, the bottom floor to video. There were more offices for white-collar workers across the street. Behind the complex, the dirty North Branch of the Chicago River flowed.

Turmell was unfazed by the change in scenery. He immediately went to work on his first coin-op game, discussing his ideas and asking around about the hardware. He had come to Midway with a chief imperative: He wanted to channel *Robotron: 2084* and *Crystal Quest*'s influence into his own twin-stick shooter.

Working at Williams offered a sharp contrast to Turmell's hours of solitude in the basement. Instead of having to do everything by himself, Turmell would now lead a team that would execute his vision. Williams had an incredibly talented pool of designers, programmers, artists, engineers, technicians, and testers working in close quarters. Developers moved between groups and games, trading knowledge and making every product a shared effort. While Turmell was not entirely welcome (even if he never caught onto it), everyone answered his technical questions and helped him get him acclimated. The sense of community was palpable.

One of Turmell's key tasks was finding an artist for his project. He ended up co-signing the hiring of John Tobias, a nineteen-year-old who had drawn *The Real Ghostbusters* comic books and dabbled in computer graphics. Tobias was new to video games, but he showed exceptional talent. To Tobias's surprise, Turmell was genuinely interested in listening to his ideas and taking them seriously.

The Running Man, Arnold Schwarzenegger's tongue-in-cheek sci-fi flick about a deadly game show, had just come out, so Turmell and Tobias batted around a game with a similar concept. They were going to make a shooter set in another futuristic game show where you had to kill hordes of enemies to win prizes and stay alive. Tobias sketched a Richard Dawson-inspired game show host with a funky suit jacket, a blonde perm, and a sleazy smile. Turmell loved the drawing, and *Smash T.V.* was born.

At first, Tobias tried to use *Narc*'s digitization technology to capture characters, but since *Smash T.V.* would have an overhead point-of-view, setting up cameras to properly film from that perspective would be impossible. That concept was scrapped in favor of Tobias's exceptional hand-drawn art.

In his entire time programming games for computers and consoles, Turmell had been hamstrung by limited hardware capabilities and meager memory sizes. Designing simple games was a necessity because he lacked access to any real horsepower. When Turmell saw Williams's proprietary arcade hardware, he rejoiced. This was the kind of top-of-the-line technology that everyone else was trying to emulate. Arcade games could run at a smooth 60 frames per second—a major upgrade over the 30 frames per second rate Turmell knew too well. Coin-op games were going to be easier to program. Within a few weeks of development, Turmell had an enemy grunt moving around the playfield. Before long, he was finding ways to push the arcade hardware to its limits.

Set in the dangerous year of 1999, *Smash T.V.* was, in its own words, "the most violent game show of all time." You played as one of two buff and heavily armed contestants gunning down hordes of opponents from room to room. Unlike *Robotron*, where all enemies on screen at the start, fresh waves of enemies would gradually enter through doors around the screen. The game was violent and chaotic. If you survived, all sorts of treasures awaited, including a "sleek 1999 Roadster," a "fabulous riding mower," a "brand new toaster," and "good meat." Actor Paul Heitsch voiced the smug host, power-up or objective for players to work toward. Rivett always liked putting smoke effects into games so he shared an idea. "It would be cool if we could put smoke trails on the ball and set it on fire when something cool happens," he said. Over lunch on plastic trays, the two sketched out what would become *NBA Jam*'s "on fire" mode.

"He's heating up!" New York Knicks commentator Marv Albert used that phrase when a player would sink shot after shot. In that spirit, *NBA Jam* would come to describe players as "heating up" when they made two shots in a row, then "on fire" after three. The third basket would torch the hoop and send up a ring of smoke. The next time you had possession, you didn't dribble an ordinary Spalding but instead an orange-hot fireball. When you launched the ball, flames sizzled and smoke billowed.

Being "on fire" meant that your shooting percentage was vastly improved and you moved with unlimited Turbo. Suddenly giving one player such an advantage heightened the stakes. If you were on fire, you wanted to maximize the mode by scoring as much as possible. Meanwhile, your opponent needed to mount an immediate comeback and put out the fire with a basket of their own. Anyone could pick up *NBA Jam* and dunk like a champ, but only the elite kept catching fire.

But at first, "on fire" was neither balanced nor well-received. When Turmell and Rivett returned from lunch, Turmell asked Sal DiVita to make him some fire graphics for the mode. DiVita didn't just think the idea was too show awkward and overcomplicated it would be. The concept was scrapped.

"Never go backwards. Keep giving them something cooler and cooler." Jarvis hammered that lesson into Turmell during the making of *Smash T.V.* Turmell was always on, always working and thinking about his latest game, sometimes through lunch. At Midway, this often meant fast food: perhaps Brown's Chicken, KFC, or the Little Caesars Pizza in a nearby Kmart. One afternoon, Turmell and Jamie Rivett walked over to Burger King when an epiphany would strike.

Rivett was a talented Australian programmer previously from Beam Software, which developed home ports of *Smash T.V.* Turmell was so impressed by the quality of the Super Nintendo port—which the tiny team at Beam created out of art assets, a cabinet on-site for reference, and zero source code—that he helped bring Rivett to Midway. On *NBA Jam*, Rivett had several responsibilities, including designing the user interface, building the glossy broadcast-style score popups, and making sure the camera moved correctly. Turmell insisted on maximum speed and responsiveness. While competitors' games ran at 30 frames per second, *NBA Jam* would move at a silky-smooth 60 frames per second. Even the menus had to keep players engaged by using flashing graphics and satisfying sound effects.

Crossing through a baseball field on their way to Burger King, Turmell and Rivett brainstormed features they could add to the game. They needed another delivering lines like "Good luck! You'll need it!" and "Big money! Big prizes! I love it!"

Turmell was eager to hear how Eugene Jarvis felt about *Smash T.V.* and showed him one of the game's death scenes. When you finally destroyed Mutoid Man—a gigantic half-man, half-tank—a modest amount of gore sprayed from the boss' body. "Yeah, I like it," Jarvis mused, "but it needs a hundred times more blood." Also, Turmell needed way more enemies per level. Based on the measly numbers he had so far, skilled players would clear *Smash T.V.* in no time. Taking this feedback to heart, Turmell multiplied the enemies exponentially and turned Mutoid Man's defeat into a Las Vegas fountain of blood.

Jarvis quickly came to have a more pronounced influence on *Smash T.V.* Williams's business model meant that all resources were poured into developing only two or three games at once, and Williams couldn't afford downtime between releases, so developers often floated from one team to another. Six months in, *Smash T.V.* was chugging through production alongside *Trog* and *Strike Force* when Lou Nicastro paid the developers a visit and put a tantalizing incentive on the table. The Williams boss would give $40,000 to the heads of the first development team to finish their game. Turmell had never picked up on any bad vibes from his fellow developers when he joined Williams, but the tone changed when this prize was dangled in front of them. Everybody who had been sharing feedback and technical

57

knowledge with Turmell started working solely on their own projects.

Turmell was still intent on winning, though, so he had to get creative. The solution was to invite Jarvis to join the project in exchange for a cut of the winnings—an offer Jarvis accepted. Turmell, Tobias, Jarvis, and the team completed *Smash T.V.* two months before *Trog* and *Strike Force*.

The resulting game was a cathartic form of sensory overload. John Tobias's semi-realistic art style complemented Jon Hey's propulsive soundtrack, which itself was frequently muffled by gunfire and explosions. Coupled with responsive controls, comical violence, and a memorable premise, *Smash T.V.* had all the building blocks of a hit. When the game went on wide release, it even sold as well as *Narc*.

The development and success of *Smash T.V.* gave the Williams crew a newfound affection for Turmell. George Petro, who was unknowingly a fan of Turmell's because of his game *Beer Run*, grew close with him. The team embraced his big personality and respected his knowledge of game design. Jarvis got to know Turmell for his desire to constantly improve his games, as well as his distinct turns of phrase; if something was a disaster, it was, in Turmell's words, "a total debacle."

For Turmell, working with Jarvis was an eye-opening experience. Jarvis had the remarkable ability to condense a problem to its core elements and say just the right thing. He knew every trick there was to making a hit coin-op game. Similarly, Jarvis was impressed by Turmell's creativity, technical ability, and work ethic. Once idol and fan, Jarvis and Turmell became mentor and student, and soon friends, too.

Smash T.V. did not come without controversy, however. One of the lures Turmell left in the game to keep players interested was the Pleasure Dome. If you finished the game, you were presented with a prompt indicating that there were still more items hidden in the studio. "If you use the keys to explore all of the secret rooms, you will find the Smash T.V. Pleasure Dome," the text read. "Once there, several of our lovely showgirls will promote you to the rank of Grand Champion!"

Hardcore players devoted their time, effort, and (most importantly) quarters to inspecting every corner of *Smash T.V.* looking for the fabled keys but never had any luck. There was one significant impediment: The Pleasure Dome never existed. Once more, Turmell wanted to give players something compelling to work toward without actually implementing the feature.

Players who had exhausted every route complained to arcade operators about the issue, who in turn hit Williams with angry letters and confused phone calls. Where was the Pleasure Dome in *Smash T.V.* and why could no one reach it? Under pressure from management, Turmell and his team programmed in the keys and a special room overflowing with models and money. Midway hastily burned and mailed out revised boards of the game.

Turmell was amused by the kerfuffle, but George Petro was baffled as to why he would tease this secret if he never had any intention of delivering. "What? It doesn't exist?" Petro said when he learned the truth about the Pleasure Dome. "Next thing you're going to tell me, the Artesians in *Beer Run* don't exist."

Turmell grinned. He had bad news.

•

In a remote desert in what looked to be the Middle East, two soldiers stood outside a bio-nuclear facility. Before storming the scene, they stopped to receive their orders via an in-game prompt: "ENTER AKHBOOB'S TOP SECRET FACILITY AND DESTROY HIS CAPABILITY TO CREATE MUTANT LIFE FORMS. YOU MUST THEN FIGHT AND CAPTURE HIM. ENTER SECRET PATH FOR BIG KEY BONUS."

Underneath those instructions was more text— something peeking through the fourth wall:

EAT AT BROWNS
BULLS RULE NOW
PISTONS WILL RULE
THE NBA AGAIN.
MIDWAY RULES

This was just how things worked at the newly christened Williams Bally/Midway. It was completely acceptable to use a screen in your own game to pros-elytize about fast food (in this case, Brown's Chicken), announce how great your company was, and talk trash to your coworkers.

For all his California flash, Mark Turmell was still a Michigan kid at heart—a fact evidenced best by his love for the Detroit Pistons. In 1991, the Pistons were in the midst of a fierce rivalry with the Chicago Bulls, and Turmell was more than happy to show his loyalty behind enemy lines. The "Motor City Bad Boys" squad led by Isiah Thomas and Bill Laimbeer won back-to-back NBA championships in 1989 and 1990. As a result, Turmell started walking around in Pistons gear, chanting "Bad boys, bad boys" in the office, much to the ire of the many Bulls fans. No taunt was better than using a screen in *Total Carnage* to swear that the Pistons would find a way to be back on top.

After *Smash T.V.*, Turmell and John Tobias went to work on a sequel of sorts. Cribbing its title from a line in *Smash T.V.*, *Total Carnage* was a farcical twist on the Gulf War starring the comically evil General Akhboob from the fictional country of Kookistan. Akhboob insisted that his Kookistani factories were only making baby milk when they were, in fact, manufacturing weapons (a timely reference to a Saddam Hussein news story of the time). Playing as two American commandos with massive biceps and bigger guns, your task was to take down Akhboob's empire by any means necessary.

Akhboob had a comically over-the-top voice, which had been supplied by a young programmer named Ed Boon.

As of late, Tobias had been itching to do more. He had been reading books on story structure and thinking about applying classic storytelling methods to an arcade game. One of his initial ideas for *Total Carnage* involved the world being invaded by ghouls from a dimension called Outworld. But adding any nuance to *Total Carnage* required Tobias to make choices about characters and themes that he couldn't sell to Turmell. Tobias found that Turmell's reaction was, for the most part, that no one cared about those things. Turmell's priorities were mechanics and gameplay—whatever he needed to do to elicit a positive reaction from the player.

But when *Total Carnage* hit arcades in January 1992, the game was received poorly, with neither players nor operators taking to it. The game was difficult but lacked the satisfying rhythms of *Smash T.V.* Instead of blasting your way out of a confined space, your goal was to gradually move up the screen to your destination, and the mechanic just wasn't as intriguing. The title also deterred operators from buying the game. It was one thing for a game to offer playful violence, it was another to expect something called *Total Carnage* to fly in bowling alleys and family entertainment centers.

Williams Bally/Midway needed to sell around 2,000 cabinets to break even on an arcade game. *Total Carnage* didn't even hit that number. After the game bombed, the company decided that the twin-stick shooter appealed to a small population of players and moved away from the genre.

Tobias and Turmell ended their creative partnership. Tobias began talking to Ed Boon, who recently programmed on *High Impact Football*, about doing a fighting game in the mold of *Street Fighter II*. During late nights at Midway, Tobias and his martial artist friends Daniel Pesina and Rich Divizio started putting together a project that drew from martial arts flicks and East Asian mythology yet added a new level of realistic violence only digitization could provide. Tobias was finally going to get to write the kind of story he wanted

Turmell was much less confident about what to do next. Although the two remained friends, losing Tobias's stellar artistic talent was a professional blow to Turmell. After all those years of his games getting bigger and better, *Total Carnage* was Turmell's first total debacle.

George Petro was wandering the halls of Midway when he noticed Turmell in his office slouching in his chair, despondent and drained. Even slumped over, he was so tall you couldn't miss him. Petro went in to cheer him up.

"What am I going to do?" Turmell said. "I don't have any good ideas." Once an arcade game bombed, there wasn't much you could do but move on to the next. As always, he was open to suggestions.

Petro stopped to think about what direction Turmell could take next. A moment later, he had the answer.

"You need to do basketball."

CHAPTER 4:
"HE'S HEATING UP"

ON A WARM CALIFORNIA NIGHT in June 1991, a big toe threatened to stop history.

Game 5 of the 1991 NBA Finals pitted the Los Angeles Lakers against the Chicago Bulls. Led by Magic Johnson, the Lakers reflected the remnants of the championship-era Showtime team, their best years behind them. They had a powerful core but were severely understaffed, with James Worthy and Byron Scott both out with injuries. Now, the best-of-7 series was Bulls 3, Lakers 1. This game at the Great Western Forum in Inglewood was LA's last chance to keep Chicago from winning the franchise's first championship.

On the other bench, a team was just beginning to peak. Winning 61 of the 82 games in a season, the Chicago Bulls had just swept former champions the Detroit Pistons in the Eastern Conference Finals. Scottie Pippen, Horace Grant, John Paxson, and Bill Cartwright were key players on a skilled and highly motivated team, but no single factor would determine Game 5 more than Michael Jordan.

After landing awkwardly on his right foot in Game 3, Jordan was suffering from a toe that reporter Ahmad Rashad described as "badly bruised and extremely painful." But nothing was going to stop Jordan from winning the trophy: not the Pistons, not the Lakers, not Magic, and not a wounded toe.

The competition was intense all evening. By the end of the third quarter, the game was tied at 80-80. Backed by Pippen and Paxson, Jordan pushed the pace, shifting the momentum in the Bulls' favor. As the final seconds of regulation ticked away, Magic Johnson launched a three-pointer. Even if he had made the shot, the points would have been statistically useless. Jordan blocked Magic anyway. Final score: Bulls 108, Lakers 101.

The Chicago locker room erupted into ecstasy. Soaked in sweat and champagne, veins rippling at his temples, and a "Bulls 1991 World Champions" cap barely clinging to his head, Michael Jordan bowed and wrapped an arm around the Larry O'Brien Championship Trophy. He squeezed and kissed the trophy like a father reuniting with a missing child. Jordan was on top of the world.

The locker room celebration from Game 5 was one of many indelible images of Michael Jordan taken in the 1990s. Under his leadership, the Chicago Bulls spent the decade running the NBA, with Jordan dominating basketball in every meaningful way.

For example, slam dunks existed before MJ, but Jordan executed his dunks with enough finesse and frequency that he cemented them as the coolest thing about basketball. To top off his winning performance in the 1987 Slam Dunk Contest, Jordan glided from the free throw line to the hoop like a jet leaving the tarmac.

The NBA and its players had long partnered with sponsors, but Jordan brokered blockbuster deals left and right, selling T-shirts and sneakers, sports drinks and cereal, hot dogs and underwear, a cartoon on Saturday morning TV, and a big-budget movie on cinema screens. Even his silhouette became iconic. Jordan's success elevated not just his own brand but also the league itself. Already popular before, NBA basketball became must-see television, and lucrative licensing deals boomed.

But for the other 26 teams in the NBA and their fans, Michael Jordan and the Bulls were not heroes. They were the antagonists that needed to be pushed off their pedestal. In the early 1990s, the league was rich with contenders.

On the Utah Jazz, John Stockton and Karl Malone weaponized stealth and strength. Clean-cut and unassuming, Stockton liked to pickpocket his opponents, run the floor, and pass the ball to Malone; Malone's bodyguard shoulders would clear the lane and smash the rim with the force of an earthquake.

On the Seattle SuperSonics, Shawn Kemp was a thunderbolt of a power forward, his step almost spring-loaded. When he jumped up to dunk (which was often), he jammed with the creativity of a kid playing on a jungle gym. There was nothing anyone could do to stop him.

Outstanding centers were plentiful: Hakeem Olajuwon, David Robinson, Patrick Ewing, Dikembe Mutombo, Alonzo Mourning. Young players like Glen Rice and Larry Johnson showed phenomenal talent. The taunts, trash talk, and physical play flowed. The Phoenix Suns' Charles Barkley was ferocious and fearless—but definitely not a role model. On the Detroit Pistons, Isiah Thomas and Bill Laimbeer tried to recapture their former glory. On the Indiana Pacers, Reggie Miller ran his mouth, then let his ruthless threes do the talking. On the Atlanta Hawks, Dominique Wilkins dunked as if he was dancing on thin air. Down in Florida, a whirlwind of a rookie was destroying backboards and egos. As the new face of the Orlando Magic, Shaquille O'Neal oozed charisma and skill, entertaining both as a player and personality alike.

Even in the midst of competition, everyone bonded in a moment of national unity. At the 1992 Summer Olympics, the best in American basketball converged in Barcelona to form the Dream Team. The combination of Magic Johnson, Larry Bird, Jordan, Pippen, Ewing, Barkley, Robinson, Stockton, Malone, and others was too much for any other country to contain. America celebrated as what was likely the single greatest basketball team to ever exist cruised to Olympic gold.

Those days were a blur of Starter jackets and Champion jerseys, VHS tapes and *Inside Stuff* episodes,

Starting Lineup action figures and Fleer trading cards. The rousing brass of "Roundball Rock" by John Tesh welcomed you to the *NBA on NBC*. Pro ball was in full bloom. It was the right moment for a big video game.

•

James Cameron stared at the television. On the screen in front of him, Max Force and Hit Man, the anti-heroes of *Narc*, strutted the streets of a virtual Chicago for another round of splattering drug pushers with guns and rocket launchers. The game's over-the-top action was the kind of thing that would entertain the hell out of teenage boys. But in a conference room in Los Angeles, George Petro, Jack Haeger, and other employees of Williams Bally/Midway prayed that *Narc* would strike a chord with one of the hottest directors in Hollywood. Cameron was the man behind what was sure to be one of the biggest movies of 1991: *Terminator 2: Judgment Day*.

Representatives from Williams Bally/Midway and Acclaim Entertainment had flown into California to meet with Cameron, producer Lawrence Kasanoff, and the Carolco Pictures contingent. The guests' goals were threefold: Acclaim wanted to make *T2* console games, Williams wanted to make the *T2* pinball game, and Midway wanted Petro and Haeger to lead the team that would use *Narc*'s digitization technology to make a *T2* arcade game.

This was just the sort of monster license Williams Bally/Midway could use as it was finding its footing in video again, and the movie was guaranteed to have the kind of futuristic imagery that would inspire a good game. To help sell Cameron on the tech, the Midway team brought along a tape featuring *Narc* gameplay and behind-the-scenes footage explaining how they created games out of actors against a blue screen. Cameron watched the screen intently. Everyone was waiting to hear what he had to say.

"You guys are making movies like I am," Cameron observed. "This is an awesome character study of motion." Then, he leapt up and turned to his staff, and said, "Give these guys everything they need!" The guests took a deep breath.

James Cameron and the Midway crew spent the evening chatting and throwing out ideas for the *T2* coin-op game. The guests got to read a confidential copy of the script. On Cameron's insistence, they visited special effects wizard Stan Winston in his studio. On the group's flight back to Chicago, George Petro returned with a strange piece of carry-on luggage: a prop Terminator head straight from Winston's shop.

Cameron was so smitten that he granted not just all three licenses but unprecedented access to the film's actors and props. Soon enough, the Midway staffers were on set, viewing dailies and building their first-person shooter game alongside the movie. When Robert Patrick wasn't playing the cold-blooded T-1000 for the film, Midway was stealing him away to a back room to digitize him for the game's final showdown. Once the project was finished, a *Terminator 2* arcade cabinet even made it to the movie's red-carpet premiere.

Released in October 1991, Midway's *Terminator 2: Judgment Day* was a roaring success, selling a whopping 11,000 units. For the first time in a long time, the industry was taking note of what Midway was doing. No one was creating graphics as real and polished as theirs—at home or in the arcade. Digitization was clearly the element that would set their games apart. In the wake of *Terminator*'s numbers, Midway management had a new philosophy, too: If you wanted your game approved, you needed to try to get a license.

Because of this, John Tobias and Ed Boon tried to snag a marquee name for their fighting game. They batted around the idea of building their project around Jean-Claude Van Damme, but the action star was out of their price range. As a cost-effective substitute, they created characters of their own. Using costumes and make-up, Tobias and Boon transformed local martial artists into ninjas, gods, and mercenaries battling in a violent tournament for the fate of Earthrealm. In six months, Tobias, Boon, John Vogel, and Dan Forden made *Mortal Kombat*.

Mark Turmell, meanwhile, moved away from blood. George Petro's suggestion about doing a basketball game had real potential. *Arch Rivals* established that there was a serious market for arcade hoops, and games with head-to-head two-player modes were the latest trend. The sports genre was fertile ground at the company, too. After *Narc*, Eugene Jarvis worked with Boon on *High Impact Football*, a violent and unlicensed football game built on digitization. While *High Impact* was not a major game sales-wise, it indicated that there was room for them to do much more with the technology.

First, Turmell sorted out the basics. How would the game play? What would it look and feel like? He knew he wanted it to be fast and fluid, so doing a two-on-two game like *Arch Rivals* would be easier to play and program than one that was five-on-five. And like *Arch Rivals*, his game would have an isometric, TV-style perspective and allow a solo player to pass to a computer-controlled teammate. Indeed, *Arch Rivals* and its success established the blueprint of how to do arcade basketball, but Turmell wanted to make his game different. For one, Turmell's game would have four player stations instead of two. Depending on which stations' Start buttons were pressed, players could play side-by-side or against each other. With four stations, four periods of play, and a suggested price of 50 cents per period, a cabinet could earn up to $8 in about ten minutes.

To make his game come to life, Turmell built a development team and recruited local basketball players to perform moves against a blue screen. Once the images of the players were inserted into the game and animated, the actors became playable characters moving around a court. Turmell showed the work-in-progress project to Neil Nicastro, his new boss. Nicastro was impressed with the game, but had a question: "Why can't we put real player heads in there?" Turmell dismissed the idea. How were they ever going to get an NBA license? For that matter, how were they going to give each player his own distinct likeness? But Nicastro stood firm: The game needed real heads.

Turmell let the feedback percolate, and soon he started to like it. No previous video game had incorporated NBA players' real faces into gameplay to any level of detail, but with Midway's tools and talent, they could figure out a way to make it work. Turmell also thought that *Arch Rivals*'s art style was too cartoony for the tone of his project. He wanted a game that was slick and lush, something that would make gamers feel like they were playing a broadcast pro match in a packed house. Putting NBA teams and logos everywhere would shoot the game's marketability into the stratosphere.

The real trick, of course, was securing the license to make this vision possible. As was often the case at Williams Bally/Midway, the task fell on Roger Sharpe.

In his early forties, with a big, bushy, black mustache, wireframe glasses, and white sneakers whether the occasion was casual or business, Sharpe had spent his life around coin-op games. Growing up in Chicago, then moving to New York City, he always harbored a special affection for pinball. He was constantly on the hunt for tables, even when playing the game was against the law.

In 1942, New York City Mayor Fiorello La Guardia had banned pinball and had 2,500 games destroyed to create one ton of scrap metal for the World War II effort. La Guardia described pinball as an "evil" that robbed the "pockets of schoolchildren in the form of nickels and dimes given them as lunch money." For over three decades, pinball remained illegal in New York City until the Music and Amusement Association convinced the city council to re-examine the ban in 1976.

The Association's star witness was Sharpe, then a journalist and expert player. Sharpe played a game and called his difficult shots as he made them, proving that it was indeed a game of skill. On that day, Roger Sharpe saved pinball, with his performance convincing the council to overturn the ban. In pinball circles, the story turned him into a folk hero.

Sharpe had a vast resume. He worked in advertising copywriting, then publishing. He edited *Video Games Magazine* and *GQ*, and wrote the 1977 book *Pinball!* He even designed pinball games of his own, like 1981's *Barracora* for Williams. When Williams and Bally/Midway merged in 1988, Sharpe became the company's licensing manager and marketing director. He managed marketing campaigns, press relationships, and licensing projects. It was Sharpe who facilitated Williams Bally/Midway's meeting with James Cameron when he said yes to *Terminator 2*. Sharpe was soft-spoken, articulate, and principled—exactly the kind of ambassador Midway needed.

Sharpe's counterpart at the NBA was Michele Brown. As head of non-apparel licensing, Brown supervised a broad category of products that included home decor and video games. Her job was to ensure that the league's brand was represented favorably. This meant that the NBA vetted proposals and potential partners in exhaustive detail. A company's chances of securing an NBA license partially depended on what its competition was doing. In this case, Midway was the only company pitching an arcade game.

Sharpe drew up a proposal and sent it to Brown. Soon thereafter, the two met at a summit between Midway and the NBA. Sharpe planned to use the same strategy that worked on Cameron: They were going to bring a videotape.

White text appeared on a black screen:

Potential NBA License
Demo Tape - 6/29/92
For NBA only

A narrator spoke. "Williams Electronics is currently developing an arcade-based four-player video basketball game, one which employs lifelike digitized graphics." The voice belonged to Jim Greene, the man behind Williams Bally/Midway's promotional videos. A three-dimensional basketball court appeared on the screen, and a message slammed into the foreground: "THIS IS NOT NINTENDO."

Greene showed off Midway's accomplishments in digitization. *Terminator 2: Judgment Day* allowed gamers to experience an interactive version of the hit film, complete with characters and levels right from the big screen. Meanwhile, *Super High Impact Football* boasted remarkable fidelity to its sport by featuring authentic-looking players executing actual plays in a realistic environment. Then, the picture faded to black, and Turmell's game faded in.

Two teams of two appeared: Jordan and Barkley versus Jordan and Barkley. As the players wandered a basketball court, the camera followed them. It was immediately clear how real and fleshed-out this world was. There were benches, the paint, a cloth net, a metal backboard. Fans filled the stands. The court had the grain and gleam of real hardwood, and the players scaled in proportion as they moved close to and further away from the camera. There was a lot missing (The only thing these players had in common with Jordan and Barkley were their names), but the likeness to actual basketball was uncanny—and this game was only a quarter finished.

Behind-the-scenes footage showed how the game was made. Greene started teasing features: a play-by-play announcer, coach's critiques, cutaway angles for dunks, and a first-person view for breakaways. "If granted an NBA license, we would elevate this game beyond any computer sports simulation ever done," Greene added. "Allowing players to choose their favorite team, and see and hear the names of recognizable players would be fantastic."

Brown and the NBA were impressed by Midway's work but had to pump the brakes immediately. Was this company serious about making an *arcade* game? The NBA had been allowing its license for home games for years, but it had never granted a coin-op license. Arcade games were the stuff of bars, strip clubs, peep show parlors, and other unsavory places where the league would not want its brand represented. The NBA had to pass.

Midway was in a bind. A game like *Mortal Kombat* could go on without Jean-Claude Van Damme, but there was no way Midway could make a big basketball game without the NBA. Sharpe was not surprised by the response, but he believed in the project and encouraged Turmell and his team to push forward. "Look, the game is going to happen," Sharpe told them. "Keep working at it." Turmell didn't think anything would change, but he took Sharpe at his word.

In order for Roger Sharpe to give up on a deal, one of two criteria had to be met. The licensor had to understand the full scope of Midway's proposal and not like it or the licensor and Midway could not come to terms financially. The NBA's response fulfilled neither. Sharpe got to work.

For decades, coin-op video games grappled with the perception of being a social ill, just as pinball had. To some, they were mindless wastes of time. They encouraged gambling. They were addictive scams that robbed kids of their lunch money. They were connected to the mob. Video arcades were unsupervised dens of drugs, alcohol, smoking, and bad behavior.

The stigma reverberated in the movies. For a time, an authority figure looking for bad guys or troublemaking youth in an arcade became a cliché. It even showed up in James Cameron's *Terminator 2: Judgment Day* when T-1000 went looking for John Connor. Connor was a 10-year-old credit card thief and a juvenile delinquent, so *of course* he was at the mall playing *After Burner*.

There were disputes in Chicago, too. In 1982, alderman Patrick Huels unsuccessfully sought to ban arcades in the city for anyone under eighteen because they bred gangs and drug traffic. Huels's ban never materialized, but the negativity persisted. "A lot of people are very narrow-minded and they feel that game rooms are where punks go," Gladys Georges, co-owner of the arcade chain Dennis' Place for Games, told the *Chicago Tribune* in 1987.

In the NBA's case, its concerns were particular to New York City. The league was headquartered in Olympic Tower, a 51-story-tall black slab in central Manhattan. The building just a mile from Times Square, a neon oblivion of drugs, porn, prostitutes, and crooks that *Rolling Stone* once called "the sleaziest block in America." Times Square was also home to several video arcades.

"There was incredible resistance," Sharpe recalled to me. "I needed to make a compelling case." Convincing the league that this project was worthwhile required Sharpe to give Brown a crash course on the value of arcades. He compiled all manner of research, including reports on how much arcades earned and stories on what kinds of clientele frequented them. He reassured Brown that this game would not appear in the kind of place you would find in Times Square but instead in family-friendly venues. Sharpe was hellbent on providing Brown with all the insight and reassurance she needed in order to see that making an arcade game would not hurt the league's reputation. If anything, it would help it.

Over 1992, Sharpe and Brown kept in touch. Sharpe continued to reassure Brown about the value of the game, and use case studies and newspaper clippings to support his arguments. Slowly, she warmed to the prospect. It helped that Brown and Sharpe got along well; she got a kick out of those clean white sneakers he always wore to business meetings.

As talks made headway, Brown flew to Chicago to see the Williams Bally/Midway office. She toured the factory and met Turmell, whose creativity and game design knowledge impressed her. He reminded her of a musician.

Midway also provided the NBA with another videotape. This one featured footage of family entertainment centers, bowling alleys, and other innocuous arcades where the game would appear. Arcade games were a form of recreation, not an outlet for deviance.

Eventually, the NBA gave Midway the green light. Midway paid the NBA an undisclosed sum for its license, plus a $100 royalty for every cabinet sold. Given Midway's forecasts and distribution network, the numbers were significant. Still, as a precaution, the NBA also wrote into the contract that if the game made it to any disreputable locations, the league had cause to pull the license. Midway became the first and, for now, only company to have the rights to create an NBA arcade game.

From there, it was onto a name. The NBA had been promoting its "NBA Jam Session" fan event as part of its annual NBA All-Star Weekend. But as a title on an arcade marquee, *NBA Jam Session* was too long. Someone suggested something punchier. "How about *NBA Jam*?" *NBA Jam* was two words, four syllables, not a letter wasted. The league agreed to the idea. Because *NBA Jam* was a play on an existing NBA property, the league would retain ownership of the name.

All said, Sharpe spent nine months carving out the deal. "With some level of modesty, I felt proud of myself. I was able to pull off something seen as the impossible," Sharpe recalled to me. "I thought by being relentless, somehow, I would win. Somehow, I would make the license happen."

Later that year, Sharpe ran into *VideoGames & Computer Entertainment* magazine associate editor Chris Bieniek at a convention in Las Vegas. The two got to talking, and Sharpe proudly teased what his company had coming next. "It's a sports game," he said, "but it's nothing like any sports game you've ever seen."

CHAPTER 5:
"HE'S ON FIRE!"

THE STRANGEST THING HAPPENED to Willie Morris Jr. Back in early 1992, when he was tearing up the courts of Chicago by day and bouncing a club by night, Morris was cooling off after a pickup game when a man introduced himself. He was making a video game about basketball, and he liked the way Morris played. He wanted to put him in the game. Morris thought he was joking.

But a few days later, on the invitation of Mark Turmell, Morris stood inside a warehouse rented out by Midway. He had to wear a generic blue and white uniform for his new gig. His playing surface would have nothing in common with the hardwood at the University of Illinois at Chicago where Turmell found him, or the outdoor courts where his stylish moves made him a local streetball hero.

Instead, he walked onto a looming blue backdrop. On set, his spectators would consist of hot lights and an elaborate network of cameras and computers. Morris would spend that afternoon and many more to come performing basketball drills—every possible move the *NBA Jam* crew could capture. His coaches consisted of Midway staffers like Turmell and video artist John Carlton.

Standing on a taped marker in the shape of an asterisk, Morris faced the camera and dribbled steadily. On a cue, he turned from one taped line to another, dribbling the same way at a new angle. He rotated his body again and dribbled a third time, then a fourth, repeating the maneuver until Midway had enough footage to simulate Morris dribbling in 360 degrees.

Morris played an entire game against an invisible opponent. He pretended to shoot, steal, pass, and block. He did layups and jump shots. He collapsed onto a gym mat like he had been pushed hard. In order for *NBA Jam* to boast a sense of realism, gamers had to perform the same motions as an actual basketball player. At 6′5″ and 198 pounds, Morris's frame gave him the prototypical body for the average NBA player. In fact, in Midway's big pitch to the NBA, it was four versions of Morris who stood in for the Jordans and Barkleys.

Like everyone else in Chicago (except Mark Turmell), Morris was a huge fan of Michael Jordan and the Chicago Bulls. Because of his marvelous moves, he earned the nickname "Air" Morris, just like his favorite player. Like Air Jordan, Air Morris knew how to get creative.

Once the Midway team finished up the fundamentals, they moved on to dunks. Using a lowered hoop as his target, Morris launched himself off a ramp over and over, attempting one highlight reel moment after another. He did the double-clutch, where he gripped the ball with both palms and pumped it into the goal; the tomahawk, where he chopped the ball in with one arm; and the windmill, where he lifted the ball up mid-air as if he was moving it from one shelf up to another.

"Let's see something different," said John Carlton. Morris took off, sitting on an invisible chair for a split second. Then, he jammed the ball in backwards. For another move, he spun his body mid-dunk as if his arms were helicopter blades, ending the rotation with a monster slam. Morris kept going, adding different angles and gestures, and Midway kept filming.

To accommodate for the differences in pro players, *NBA Jam* required both black and white skin tones, and a few body types. Turmell recruited three more amateur or college players: Todd McClearn, Tony Scott, and Stephen Howard.

Like Morris, Howard met Turmell after a pickup game. A small forward with a successful playing career at DePaul University, Howard was freshly graduated and hoped to pick up an NBA contract in the fall. As a gamer, Howard recognized the Midway name and liked Turmell's vision. Howard said yes, convincing Turmell to pay him a little extra since he was going to be a real NBA player soon, too.

Howard spent hours in the studio repeating simple poses and waiting to perform. At times, the work got monotonous. But when he had the opportunity to do something big, like a somersault dunk off a picnic table, Howard understood just how cool this game could be. Those weekend blue screen sessions laid the foundation for *NBA Jam*.

Assembling a development team at Midway was a process based on the project's needs and the employees' personal tastes alike. Turmell checked around the office to see who was available. Across 1992, a core team of seven built *NBA Jam*:

- Mark Turmell, lead designer
- Shawn Liptak, programmer
- Jamie Rivett, programmer
- John Carlton, artist
- Tony Goskie, artist
- Sal DiVita, artist
- Jon Hey, music supervisor

Roles shifted through development, and other Midway developers pitched in. Early in the process, artist and *Joust* creator John Newcomer taught Turmell the digitization techniques he learned while making *High Impact Football*, but Newcomer wasn't involved in the long-term development of *NBA Jam*.

While Newcomer brought a coin-op veteran's perspective to the project, Sal DiVita was brand new to video games. A twentysomething native of Chicago a few years younger than Turmell, DiVita always had a knack for drawing. He grew up hoping to create oil paintings for book covers and movie posters. But in the late 80s, DiVita discovered the Amiga 2000, a personal computer that allowed him to create 3D art. Turning his newfound skills into a job, he worked at a company making educational tapes with his art school friend Tony Goskie. After Goskie left the tapes company and got a job at Midway, he encouraged DiVita to apply and join him. They worked alongside one another again on *NBA Jam*.

Creative oversight at Midway was minimal. As long as a team could deliver a sellable game on a tight deadline, management left imaginations free to roam. Some members of the *NBA Jam* team were basketball fans while others never watched. Some had worked with Turmell before while others hadn't. Some expected the game to strive for realism while others were more open to interpretation. There was no shortage of skills or opinions to go around. If the game shipped early, the team would earn a twenty percent royalty bonus.

Hi-8 tape of the blue screen sessions in hand, Carlton and Goskie processed the footage on computers, then snipped the best takes and stripped the actors from the background frame by frame. While the blue background gave them great tonal range while filming, putting blue uniforms on that background was a bad decision. Cleaning up the images was a time-consuming process;

having to manually remove and adjust the tiny blue pixels clinging to the actors' outlines made it take forever.

After that, the artists isolated sections of the jerseys and created "slots" that filled with a team's colors on command. The palette swapping technique saved both memory and time; *Mortal Kombat* had used it to great effect. Customizing each team's uniform down to its logos and details was not possible, so each duo was instead differentiated by a color combination. When the Seattle SuperSonics were picked, the slots filled with green and yellow; for the Phoenix Suns, purple and orange; for the Orlando Magic, black and blue; and so on.

NBA Jam's graphics benefitted from top-shelf tech. While competitors used sixteen palettes of sixteen colors for their games, Midway's hardware provided room for 256 palettes of 256 colors, creating a lush range of shades. Turmell encouraged his artists to intensifying the brightness of the jerseys until the colors popped.

Once their bodies were sorted out, the original studio actors' heads were removed from their necks and replaced by a digital "object attach" point. As with the jerseys, different head and body combinations could seamlessly produce playable NBA characters in seconds. Turmell and sound designer Jon Hey picked the lineups, using box scores, articles, and intuition to determine which two-man squads would best represent each team. On a Team Select screen, each pro would come to be represented by a portrait, a last name, and four attributes. Although not all of their original choices were approved by the NBA (most notably, Michael Jordan), the game's final roll call was stacked.

Unlike other basketball games that had mere flashes of name-brand talent, *NBA Jam*'s 54-player roster was stuffed with the era's hottest stars. Drawing from the 1992 to 1993 season, it seemed like everyone was in there: Charles Barkley, Hakeem Olajuwon, Scottie Pippen, Shawn Kemp, Karl Malone, John Stockton, Dominique Wilkins, Reggie Miller, Glen Rice, Larry Johnson, David Robinson, James Worthy, Tim Hardaway, Shaquille O'Neal. *NBA Jam* would feature 37 former, present, and future All-Stars, including three-quarters of the Dream Team. Superstardom was just a couple of quarters away.

The artist responsible for drawing every in-game head was Tony Goskie. Armed with the program Deluxe Paint, Goskie had to do it all by hand. Since the NBA supplied Midway with only face-on shots, Goskie had to extrapolate photos and video stills to draw each of the eleven angles required of every player head. The task was even more labor-intensive than extracting the actors from the tape. Goskie spent two painstaking months just drawing the heads.

There was also the matter of designing the battle-ground. DePaul University granted Midway access to its basketball court, so Goskie headed over with a camera and shot footage from the stands. On his computer, he compiled a row of still frames into a panorama of a court, then digitally painted the whole thing into the game. The hardwood, the hoops, the backboard, the scorer's table: It all turned to pixels. Goskie gave *NBA Jam* court a blue and red scheme as a nod to both the DePaul Blue Demons and Turmell's beloved Detroit Pistons. Once the court was made, he grabbed video of real-life basketball spectators and painted the fans into the game, animating them so they reacted to *NBA Jam*'s on-court happenings appropriately. A few familiar Midway faces made it into the audience, too; Goskie himself can be spotted on the left baseline, thoughtfully stroking his chin.

In another touch of authenticity, boards along the sidelines changed ads between periods. Midway wanted to use the same sponsors as NBA television broadcasts, but the league didn't want to leverage any trademarks it didn't own. As a result, the team came up with its own sponsors. *NBA Jam* was brought to you by the likes of Tortorice's Pizzeria (a real local pizza chain), Air Morris sneakers (a fake shoe brand), Cheer-Accident (the indie rock band *Mortal Kombat* sound designer Dan Forden played in), and the inevitable *Mortal Kombat II*.

To flesh out this world, non-playable characters were also digitized. Midway developer Jake Simpson stepped in as a referee who appeared at tip-off to launch the ball and then vanished for the rest of the game. *NBA Jam* needed cheerleaders on the sidelines to supplement the on-court visual, too. On behalf of the *Jam* team, Midway artist Jack Haeger called *Playboy*'s office in Chicago to see if any models were available.

Seven miles from Williams Bally/Midway headquarters, a telephone rang. The employee who answered had no clue what Haeger was going on about, so she put Haeger on hold and turned to a coworker. "Hey Kerri," she said. "This is some weird call. Why don't you take it? It sounds like something you could do."

A beautiful blonde in her early twenties, Kerri Hoskins was a multi-talented *Playboy* employee who started her career posing for the magazine. She had risen to a behind-the-camera job hiring models and arranging shoots. Hoskins was in the middle of editing photos when she took the call. Like her coworker, she also had no clue what the gig would entail, but it sounded fun. She signed herself up, even though she had no cheerleading experience.

Since the job required two models, Hoskins made sure to bring along a colleague who would know what she was doing. Lorraine Olivia had been a cheerleader in high school and college, so when it was time for the two to perform simple routines in front of the blue screen, Olivia would perform a move and Hoskins would imitate it. The pair would also be featured in *NBA Jam*'s attract mode and ending screens. If you were able to defeat all 27 teams—a feat neither easy nor cheap—you were met with Hoskins popping champagne and Olivia raising a trophy in your honor.

Despite their initial hesitations, Hoskins (who today goes by Kerri Ann Hoskins Reavis) and Olivia (today Lorraine Hocker) enjoyed themselves at the shoots. The

Midway guys were laid-back, easy to work with, and apologetic when their slow tech would crash and delay the shoots. Once the day's obligations were met, Hoskins sometimes went out for drinks with the crew. She got to know developers who were passionately devoted to complex and time-consuming work. The developers spent their lives in the office, couches scattered around the space. When a hard deadline loomed, a developer might sit in front of his computer all day, sleep on a couch for a few hours at night, and then return to his post.

The surroundings matched the mindset. While Williams Bally/Midway was rich with world-class talent, its workspace was often raw and grungy. The smells of stale coffee and used machine oil would linger in the air. Junk food wrappers filled the garbage bins. High-voltage arcade-grade monitors that were meant to be placed inside cabinets instead sat on desks outside their enclosures, their wiring dangerously exposed.

The company's hard-nosed attitude toward churning out product was spearheaded by Neil Nicastro. Sal DiVita knew the grind of "the death march," his phrase for what we today call "crunch"—the game industry's brutal and controversial practice of pushing developers through long work weeks to ensure a game ships on time. The death march was simply a fact of life at Midway, and if he had to, Nicastro would motivate the crew by comparing them to the ancient Spartans. "We don't need any kind of luxuries," Nicastro might say, in DiVita's paraphrase. "We don't need any decadence.

We live in the trenches. We live in the dirt. Our office is a mess. Our office is disgusting, and it's going to stay that way because I don't want you thinking you can relax at any time and you're living the high life. We keep on going. You're not stars of any sort. You just fucking make games!"

Midway throbbed with the vitality of young, hungry minds tuned to the same wavelength and willing to do whatever it took to make great products. Everything was about games at Midway. If employees weren't playing each other's games, they were binging on first-person shooters. It wasn't uncommon for the workday to begin in the afternoon. Then, at night, after management went home and the developers returned from dinner, the real work would begin.

As lead designer, Turmell was there to make sure his team was content and focused. Nobody would commit to the death march if they didn't feel like their opinions mattered. Turmell saw himself as the impartial referee of the development process sorting through everyone's ideas, lobbying for the good and trashing the bad. He also focused on optimizing the game's finer points and incorporating user feedback. One of his favorite things to do was offer someone the controls and watch how they played his game. Of course, no one's opinion mattered more to Turmell than Eugene Jarvis's.

By that point, Jarvis had left Williams Bally/Midway once again to establish TV Games, Inc, a coin-op studio developing a racing game called *Cruis'n USA*. Since TV

Games still needed manufacturing and distribution, it kept close ties with Midway, meaning that Jarvis was still around the office.

John Carlton had recently finished turning Air Morris's dynamic moves into player animations. The game looked uncannily realistic. Carlton copied the animations, which included a slam dunk, to a floppy disk for Turmell. From there, Turmell moved Willie Morris Jr. around the court to get a feel for how the game would play. Nailing the responsiveness of the controls was key to getting the player engaged in the action.

Turmell showed Jarvis how good the slam dunk looked. On the screen, Morris jumped a reasonable, realistic height and rattled the rim like an NBA star. "I like it," Jarvis said, "but I think players should jump three times higher."

Now there was an idea. To make a dunk happen, Turmell programmed a calculation involving Morris jumping into the air and having his hand touch the rim. If needed, Turmell could adjust the height to which he jumped and the speed at which he took off. By playing with rotations and velocities, Morris could leap higher and higher above the hoop.

John Carlton was at his desk when the phone rang. "We've got the dunk in," Turmell said. "You want to check it out?" Carlton eagerly headed over. Everything from the digitization sessions translated flawlessly so far.

When he walked into Turmell's office, Air Morris launched from the free-throw line to what felt like twenty feet in the air, and came down with a colossal slam dunk. The move was absurd—less like something from an NBA game than its halftime show. Carlton was totally put off. "What is this?" he said. "This isn't realistic at all." "It's an *arcade* game," Turmell countered. The argument continued, but Turmell stood firm: The new dunks were staying.

Midway videographer Jim Greene was down the hallway working when he heard commotion coming from Turmell's office. He found Turmell and Sal DiVita howling with laughter as their players did one absurd dunk after another. "If you had seen it," Greene recalled to me, "you would have had two simultaneous thoughts: 'This game is going to be huge' and 'The NBA might not get the joke.'"

The team chopped up dunk animations so depending on how and where on the court you took off from, a segment from one dunk would flow into part of another. Figuring out this system took a while, but it was a breakthrough. Other Midway staffers would pop by Turmell's office to get a look at the dunks, and before long, Carlton saw the light, too. The league didn't have a problem with the feature either. The decision to keep the crazy dunks took *NBA Jam*'s aesthetic from "reality" to what DiVita described as "exaggerated reality."

If you had an opinion about the game, you had to be willing to fight for it. The tight-knit group argued over everything: how often you should be able to steal, how often you could block, what the graphics looked like. Everyone felt safe to speak honestly. "We fought like cats and dogs: screaming, throwing chairs. We were a bunch of adolescent apes in this enclosure, and we acted like animals," DiVita recalled to me. He and Turmell squabbled most of all. "I'm a Sicilian, man. I was young," DiVita said. "It was a very energetic group. We had a lot of fun together."

The game kept getting features, like an "Enter Your Initials" menu that functioned as both a leaderboard and a way to save your progress on a particular cabinet. In addition to stealing the ball the normal way, *NBA Jam* let you to outright shove your opponent, similar to how the punching mechanic worked in *Arch Rivals*. Since the team never initially planned to put shoving in the game, it improvised by recycling animation of a chest pass.

Not every idea was a winner. Inessential or difficult-to-implement ones mentioned in the pitch video were cut, like alternate angles and a vague "Coach Mode." Turmell had one clunker. Instead of dunks simply playing out as animations, he wanted to see what it would be like for players to manually adjust their height in mid-air, similar to how Super Mario could flutter up and down in flight in *Super Mario Bros. 3*. Programmer Shawn Liptak thought that this was an addition too absurd for a game absurd enough, but Turmell prodded him to try it. Liptak slapped together some code to over the top for their game but also that the mode, in its earliest form, gave the player too much of an advantage. Undeterred, Turmell resorted to reusing fire art from *Smash T.V.* to make the visual happen, and kept working on it. In time, the refined mode proved to add another element of excitement to the game. Just as with John Carlton and the dunks, DiVita soon realized how wrong he was. "On fire" would become one of *NBA Jam*'s signature elements.

While Midway's hardware had the capacity for cutting-edge visuals, the company's tools on the audio side were lacking. Jon Hey knew this well because he had been creating sound at Williams Bally/Midway for a few years before working on *NBA Jam*. Hey, a pianist with a vast and accomplished musical background, found programming video game music to be a tedious and exacting process. When he recorded voice clips for the game, he had to use continuously variable slope delta (CVSD) modulation, an outdated audio compression scheme that dated back to World War II walkie-talkies. Speech recorded in CVSD had a grainy texture.

Compared to the aggressive soundtracks for *Smash T.V.* and *Total Carnage*, Hey's work on *NBA Jam* was funkier and downright more fun. He wrote all the game's music, including its hooky title theme inspired by sports broadcast music and "(Not Just) Knee Deep" by George Clinton's band Funkadelic.

When it came to adding sounds to the on-court action, Hey decided that stock effects were too ambient for what he wanted, so he went about recording his own. Hey dribbled a basketball on different surfaces and squeaked his sneakers across floors in search of the perfect tones. He tossed in comical effects, too, like the whir of chopper blades to accompany Air Morris's helicopter dunk and a cartoonish "boi-yoing" for when a lousy shot bounced off the rim.

Hey was also responsible for making sure the game had commentary that made it feel like a TV broadcast. Turmell and Hey envisioned a play-by-play announcer who said players' names and called the action as it unfolded, and even considered hiring Marv Albert until he proved to be far out of their price range. Turmell then suggested that Hey take the announcer role because he had prior voice-over experience. Hey had another idea: What about Tim Kitzrow?

In his free time, Hey played music around Chicago, which was how he met Kitzrow, a drummer who happened to be a skilled voice actor. Born in Wisconsin and bred in Upstate New York, Kitzrow arrived in the city in 1987 with big dreams of an acting career. He was dedicated to his craft, classically trained at Purchase College in New York, and handsome like Cary Elwes. More than anything, Kitzrow loved comedy. He studied with Chicago's Second City school and attended auditions at the same time as actors like Stephen Colbert, Steve Carell, Amy Poehler, Tina Fey, and Tim Meadows. Yet while they went on to score bigger roles, Kitzrow grinded but never got that break.

By 1992, Kitzrow was in his early thirties, waiting tables and trying out for beer and deodorant ads, still certain he was destined for success. He was drumming in a rock band called the Lazy Boy Rockers for fun when Hey asked if he wanted to do a voice for a *Gilligan's Island* pinball game. Kitzrow thought it sounded fun. He nailed his impression of snobbish millionaire Mr. Howell, which led to Hey offering Kitzrow more gigs on licensed pinball games.

Kitzrow had never done a video game and knew little about the medium—in college, he spent his quarters on beer instead of *Pac-Man*—but he did know basketball. He grew up calling out last-second shots in his driveway and idolizing Kareem Abdul-Jabbar in his days on the Milwaukee Bucks. As an adult, he was a die-hard Bulls fan.

Turmell and Hey explained their vision to Kitzrow. They wanted something energetic, something over the top, something that would stand out in a noisy arcade. While *NBA Jam* required commentary, the machine's software left little space for audio files so the calls needed to be short and forceful. Luckily, the game moved so fast that shorter phrases worked better anyway. Hey wrote a script, and Turmell approved it, leaving Hey and Kitzrow to their own devices.

Midway's recording studio consisted of a sparse isolation booth nicknamed, among other things, "the meat locker." The five-foot-by-five-foot space had a window and little else. "You could sit in a chair," Hey recalled, "but I don't think Tim ever sat."

"Here's the tip!" "From downtown!" "Magic carpet ride!" "Razzle dazzle!" "Launches a shot!" "Lays it up!" "Swish!"

While *NBA Jam*'s announcer started as a riff on Marv Albert, Kitzrow's booming voice and enthusiastic delivery quickly gave it his own character. Since he didn't have any gameplay to watch for inspiration, Kitzrow imagined that he was calling playoff basketball. Memory limitations meant that *Jam* had no room for first names, so instead of saying "Shaquille O'Neal" and "the Orlando Magic," he would say "O'Neal" and "Magic." To accommodate the game's varying scenarios, he recorded each player's name with three inflections of increasing intensity: "Pippen!" "*Pippen!*" "PIPPEN!" *NBA Jam* would set itself apart with its exclamations.

"Ugly shot!" "No way!" "The turnover!" "The rebound!" "The nail in the coffin!" "Nothing but net!" "Jams it in!" "He's heating up!" "HE'S ON FIRE!"

One time, as Jon Hey manned the mixing console, artist John Carlton was sitting at his desk nearby. He was on a Sly and the Family Stone kick. He had the classic funk group's song "I Want to Take You Higher" stuck in his head, especially the one part that went "Boom-alaka-laka/Boom-alaka-laka." This inspired Carlton to roll over to Hey and make a request: "Tell him to say, 'Boomshakalaka.'"

Hey passed the message into the meat locker. "Say 'Boomshakalaka.'"

"What's 'Boomshakalaka?'" Kitzrow responded.

"Just say it," Hey said.

"BOOMSHAKALAKA!" The word thundered off Kitzrow's tongue. It was as if the slam dunk got its own onomatopoeia.

Even with his voice distorted by the CVSD compression, Kitzrow's charisma rang through as he rattled off one-liners, talked smack, and kept the hype heavy. In total, Kitzrow spent about twenty hours in the meat locker, earning somewhere between $1,000 and $1,500 for *NBA Jam*. It was a good gig.

Even more than the audiovisual components, what would ultimately most determine how much money arcade players spent on the game would be its gameplay. Programmer Shawn Liptak was crucial to shaping the technical aspects of the on-court experience. Among other things, he adjusted values to determine how often shots would land, developed a physics system to make the ball move realistically, and figured out how to make the players scale in size based on proximity to the camera. *NBA Jam* had much more than the dunks going for it. It held the possibility of layups, jumpers, and Hail Mary three-pointers, too.

Under the hood, Turmell made subtle changes, such as getting the game clock to speed up and slow down at certain intervals to affect the pace of the action. He also programmed in "wild hares," his words for surprising game behaviors triggered under rare circumstances. Most importantly, he coded in "rubber banding" percentages that would keep scores on a seesaw. In simple terms, if Team 1 had been scoring more than Team 2, *NBA Jam* would decrease Team 1's chances of scoring another shot and increase Team 2's chances of making one. Then, as Team 2 recovered, the momentum would shift back the other way to give Team 1 another chance, and on and on, stretching in and out like the elastic of a rubber band. Striking this delicate balance was key to making *NBA Jam* a compelling experience. In the spirit of *Robotron: 2084*, Turmell wanted a game where stakes were high and victories were often by razor-thin margins.

Once *NBA Jam* was complete, the team played it extensively to refine its finer points. Turmell, DiVita, Hey, and Rivett got so into the game that they gambled on it. The prizes began as snacks from the vending machine. Soon, hundreds of dollars were trading hands. Since he was accessing and tweaking the stats so often, Turmell had the best understanding of how each player performed (and also happened to win a lot).

It was important for *NBA Jam* to physically make an impact, too. Tony Goskie designed the cabinet's art, splashing a big NBA logo on its sides so you could easily identify it from a distance, even in a dark arcade like Dennis' Place for Games.

Those first nights on test at Dennis' Place were a tidal wave of good vibes. Almost immediately, *NBA Jam* attracted steady streams of huge, loud crowds that surrounded the game. DiVita witnessed one wild reaction for himself when a secret first showed its head.

In the fourth quarter of a game, one player leapt up and came down with a dunk so hard that he broke the backboard. Virtual glass shattered onto hardwood, and the NBA players collapsed in slow motion. Most memorably, the actual guy who broke the backboard couldn't believe it. "Oh, *HELL* no!" he shouted. Then, he did laps around the arcade celebrating while a crowd chased him and cheered.

NBA Jam was finished in ten months—two ahead of schedule, earning the team its twenty percent royalty bonus. Roger Sharpe created a flyer for the game, which he mailed to arcade operators and distributors around the country. Unlike the flyers for *TV Basketball* or *Arch Rivals*, Midway's latest basketball game had portraits of famous pros—Charles Barkley, Karl Malone, Reggie Miller—jumping off the glossy paper. *NBA Jam* had a tagline, too: "Altitude with an attitude!"

The game was on its way to taking over Chicago. Now, it was a matter of seeing how it would do everywhere else.

CHAPTER 6:
"BOOMSHAKALAKA!"

THE LASER PRINTER CHUGGED over and over, repeating the sound: *tzk-heet, tzk-heet, tzk-heet.*

Page after page shot out into the tray, and Randolph Vance stood close by to pick them up. A sophomore at the University of Kentucky, Vance had spent much of early 1993 in a campus computer lab writing and researching a project with his friend and fellow student William "Greg" Henderson. But with each passing crank of the printer, the death glares of the computer lab staffers grew more intense. Similarly, when Vance and Henderson used the lab's high-end NeXT computers to research their project, the people at the desk were less than pleased. But nothing was going to deter Vance and Henderson from putting together "How to WIN at *NBA JAM!*," the world's first *NBA Jam* strategy guide.

Freshly inked copies of their work stowed in their backpacks, the friends headed off campus. As was often the case, they left to spend their evenings at the Kentucky Arcade, a game room in downtown Lexington. Covered in the blue and white of the University of Kentucky Wildcats, the Kentucky Arcade was a hot spot for college kids and stayed open long past midnight. Its blacklight carpet was filled with the best in pinball and video games, including two Neo Geo cabinets, two *Street Fighter II: Champion Edition* cabinets, two *X-Men* cabinets, three *Mortal Kombat* cabinets, and, as of late, two *NBA Jam* cabinets.

The Kentucky Arcade had become one of Vance's favorite distractions. His home life was busy, with two ailing parents to care for. His mother Sigrid had a double hip replacement, and his father Virgil was a Navy veteran paralyzed on the left side. Virgil ran Van Brook of Lexington, a company that manufactured tokens for laundromats, car washes, arcades, and other businesses. Virgil was so closely associated with his products that his nickname was "the Token King." When business at Van Brook was booming, Virgil bought *Kings & Queens*, the pinball machine from the movie *Tommy*, and modified it so he could control both flippers with one hand. Randolph grew up around arcade games and trade shows, inheriting his father's love of coin-op machines.

Converting dollars into tokens stamped with the image of a wildcat, Vance and Henderson deposited the coins into *NBA Jam*. The two were spending so much money on the game, but they had never seen anything quite like it. Vance wasn't any good at fighting games because he couldn't remember any of the complex button combos so *Jam*'s intuitive three-button setup was perfect for his play style. When they played against each other, Henderson switched up teams, sometimes picking the Hawks, other times the Bulls. Vance on the other hand favored the Golden State Warriors because of their prowess at shooting three-pointers. After all, Lexington was where the Wildcats had mastered the three-pointer. Kentucky might not have had a pro team, but make no mistake: This was basketball country.

Soon after developing their *NBA Jam* obsession, Vance and Henderson began working on their Frequently Asked Questions (FAQ) guide. Building off an original guide by Carl Chavez, "How to WIN at *NBA JAM*!" was meticulously researched and always growing. The FAQ covered both basics (like getting on fire) and advanced techniques (like "milking the clock"). *NBA Jam* had become the most talked-about game in the arcade, and Paul, the Kentucky Arcade's owner, sold Vance and Henderson's printed-out copies for $2 apiece.

The document lived on rec.games.video.arcade, a newsgroup on Usenet, the bulletin-board-style precursor to the World Wide Web. The community was a lively place, rich with chatter about arcade games. While *NBA Jam* was enjoyed across the board, dedicated players vented their frustrations with the game's rubber banding and difficulty. Two posters made a list of *NBA Jam* terms they were using in an effort to get everyone else to adopt them. For example, a "goon" was someone who pushed all the time, a "squid" constantly had their arms in their opponent's real-life personal space, and a player slacking on defense was guilty of "casual D." Fans gossiped about what treasures *NBA Jam* might hold, such as the ability to play as the cheerleaders or even Michael Jordan.

Vance and Henderson's interest in *NBA Jam* first deepened when Vance saw another arcade patron controlling a player in the game he didn't recognize. He had never heard of an NBA player named "Turmell." "How'd you do that?" Vance asked the stranger. All you had to do to play as Turmell, he explained, was enter MJT as your initials and March 22 as your birthday in the "Enter Your Initials" menu.

The next time the friends were up, they tried the code. It worked—and this Turmell guy was a great player, too. Soon, they ran into another code. Entering WIL, January 1 unlocked another mysterious character, this one named Air Morris. At that point, they were certain there had to be more secrets buried in the game.

Vance couldn't stop thinking about this Turmell character. He deduced that the player was an avatar of Mark Turmell, the *NBA Jam* developer whose name and face Vance recognized in the game's attract mode. Tracking down Turmell might be the key to more codes.

Before long, Vance and Henderson were at the University of Kentucky library tracking down a Chicago phone book. Cracking open the T's, they scanned the lines of text until they hit their target: "TURMELL, MARK JOSEPH."

They dialed the number. At a residence in Chicago, a phone rang.

"Hello?" the man said. Vance and Henderson quickly explained who they were and why they were calling. They were working on an *NBA Jam* guide and wanted to know more about the codes, and they knew he worked on the game so maybe he had more info to share. Turmell was peeved that they had called his home number, but he understood the pressing need for the information. "Call me at work and we can talk about them then," Turmell said, giving them his work number.

A few days later, Vance and Henderson spoke to Turmell again. Not only was Turmell happy to share another code—enter SAL, February 1 to play as Sal DiVita—but he was willing to talk a third time.

For weeks, the conversations happened at a steady clip, and Turmell's work phone turned into Vance and Henderson's private *NBA Jam* hotline. Typically, Turmell would ask how the game was performing at the Kentucky Arcade, they would chit-chat, and then he would reveal another nugget. Enter GNP, October 8 to play as George Petro; HOW, July 15 for Stephen Howard; TWG, December 7 for Tony Goskie; and so on. Some calls lasted a few minutes. Others, an hour. Each one meant another update to the strategy guide.

Vance and Henderson stuffed the two *NBA Jam* machines with tokens, meeting one new player after another and always hunting for more. Notebooks in hand, they tested long lists of potential code combinations to find rumored characters, marking off incorrect guesses as they went along. With its frequent updates and authoritative tone, "How to WIN at *NBA JAM!*" became the must-read text file of 1993.

Chris Bieniek was also on the prowl for *NBA Jam* codes. Readers were writing to *VideoGames & Computer Entertainment*, the magazine he edited, looking for the inside scoop on *Jam*. Other magazines were bound to pick up on *NBA Jam* mania, but no one had published a *Jam* strategy guide yet. *VG&CE* had a strong working relationship with Midway (it broke the news about *Mortal Kombat*'s secret character, Reptile) so Roger Sharpe put Bieniek in touch with Mark Turmell directly. Turmell revealed how you could play as all seven members of the *NBA Jam* development team, a scoop which ran in its June 1993 issue. Bieniek knew there was tremendous value in running more extensive coverage, so Turmell had a suggestion. "You know, there's an FAQ out there written by a couple of fans. You should check it out," he said, offering to fill any gaps afterward.

Bieniek had never even heard of a FAQ before, but when he saw the guide on Usenet, it was exactly what he was looking for. *VideoGames & Computer Entertainment* reached out and made an offer. Vance and Henderson, and later Carl Chavez, each received $200 for the rights to adapt "How To WIN at *NBA Jam!*" into a magazine article.

On the August 1993 issue of *VG&CE*, a shot of an *NBA Jam* cabinet and a strange screenshot of the game popped out of the cover. Inside, a colorful eleven-page spread called "The Secrets of *NBA JAM*" broke down how to master the game and access its hidden features. Thirteen of the secret characters (or, as the guide called them, "special guests") were sealed in the posterity of print.

Vance and Henderson had worked around the clock to fact-check every code and make sure everything made it into the guide, and seeing their results in this new format was immensely gratifying. Vance recognized his own phrasing in the text; they even left in the shout-out to the Kentucky Arcade. His parents were impressed that they had a writer in the house, even if they had no clue what anything he wrote meant.

The early summer months dedicated to playing, writing, and talking about the game were fun for Vance and Henderson, but the two still had miles left to go on their *NBA Jam* journey—specifically, 380 of them, pointed north toward Chicago.

•

For a second there, Mark Turmell thought *NBA Jam* might fail.

At one point when the game was on test, it was competing against *Run & Gun*, Konami's unlicensed but impressive 3D basketball game. The threat the game posed to *NBA Jam* scared him. He noticed that arcade players who looked like they actually played ball gravitated toward *Run & Gun*. Turmell resigned himself to the notion that legitimate ballers liked Konami's game better than his game, but that feeling couldn't have lasted for more than a week or two. When it got going, *NBA Jam* took off—*fast*.

The public at large got its first real taste of the game in February 1993 at the NBA All-Star Weekend in Salt Lake City, Utah. The Jam Session fan event at the Delta Center made the ideal spot for a special NBA Jam Session Video Arcade. Two long rows of *NBA Jam* machines fresh off Midway's production line were mobbed by basketball fans from around the country. A Midway camera crew drifted around the arcade capturing footage of players sampling the game and quickly getting into it. They met one teenager pumping his fist and celebrating a moment of triumph. "This is *bad*, man!" the teen said, using that word in its most 90s sense possible. "This is bad!"

The NBA was blown away by the game and its reception, too. "It legitimized the whole arcade category for us," NBA licensing director Michele Brown recalled. "This was the next best thing to playing on the court or attending a game. You're playing coach and you're playing the player."

As the game went into wide release, the crowds grew bigger and bigger, and earnings skyrocketed. The money the game was making in Chicago alone was crazy. In one arcade, *NBA Jam* experienced a problem of *Pong*-like proportions: It made so much money that the cash box needed to be routinely emptied or the machine would stop working. Arcade operators griped that Midway hadn't built the cash box to be big enough.

Chicago was also where the game broke a record. During the week of July 4, 1993, *NBA Jam* earned a staggering $2,468 at the Dennis' Place for Games on West Lawrence Avenue. Turmell heard that this was the most money made by an arcade game in a single week. Marcus Webb, editor of the coin-op business magazine *RePlay*, speculated that *NBA Jam* "may be, on a week-by-week basis, the best-earning video game in the history of the industry." On *RePlay*'s Player's Choice monthly chart, which tracked how coin-op games were earning, *NBA Jam* reigned at the no. 1 spot from April through November.

"The summer of 1993 was like the summer of *NBA Jam*," Chris Bieniek recalled to me. At *VideoGames & Computer Entertainment* magazine, the *NBA Jam* hysteria was clear. On top of Vance and Henderson's guide, the August '93 issue of *VG&CE* featured a contest to win an *NBA Jam* cabinet of your own, courtesy of Midway. People sent in enough postcards to fill a bag the size of an industrial waste bin liner. Bieniek and his colleagues hauled the sack to a convention so Turmell could stick his hand in and pick the winner himself. As it so happened, a kid from Illinois mailed the lucky entry, so Midway shipped a machine straight from the factory to his door.

Around that time, another journalist named Dan Amrich started his mornings with *NBA Jam*. Shortly before being hired at the popular video game magazine *GamePro*, where he became better known as Dan Elektro, he wrote for music and basketball mags in New York City. His commute involved daily trains from New Jersey to Manhattan, a journey that often included a stop at Station Break, a massive subterranean arcade just under Madison Square Garden in Penn Station. The machines were always in use, but Amrich would try to grab a game of *Jam* on one of its several cabinets. He was smitten with how the game offered a rare cooperative coin-op experience. "*NBA Jam* really rewarded players who worked together," Amrich said. "Unlike fighting games, where the experience was always competitive and short, here you could put in enough quarters for a full game and work with another player for twelve minutes."

On the opposite side of the country, Jon Robinson— the future *GamePro* writer/editor Johnny Ballgame— first saw *NBA Jam* at a mall arcade in the Bay Area. The game had just come out, but players were already shouting lines like "BOOMSHAKALAKA!" and "Is it the shoes?" across the floor. "I look at *Jam* as the first sports battle game," Robinson said to me. "There's nothing better than playing against a guy and letting him know that you knocked out three three-pointers in a row, basically shoving it in his face in front of the arcade. That's what *Jam* was: the most trash-talking game in the arcade."

NBA Jam's most impressive fans were the players featured in the game itself. David Robinson, Shawn Kemp, Mark Price, and Derek Harper were avid fans. Artist Tony Goskie learned firsthand about the game's reach when he bumped into Patrick Ewing, the 7-foot-tall New York Knicks star, in an airport gift shop. When Goskie introduced himself to Ewing as the man who drew his likeness for *NBA Jam*, his art evidently wasn't up to standard. Ewing grabbed Goskie by the shirt and jokingly threatened him, saying, "You're the one who did me wrong."

On the court, Glen Rice was a three-point sharp-shooter on the Miami Heat flourishing into an NBA All-Star. But at an arcade in Miami, he was just another player braving the long lines for his turn at the game. "I was an *NBA Jam* junkie," Glen Rice told me. Once the hassle got to be too much, he simply bought a cabinet of his own. "That game was addicting," he said. "It was like your favorite piece of candy. You couldn't get enough of it."

Rice took his *Jam* seriously. At its peak, he would play the game until three o' clock in the morning. He always picked the same team (the Heat) and the same player (himself). "I was good, too. I was really good. I would always tell people, 'Listen, let me play me. I know how to work me,'" he said. "I was *the* Glen Rice on top of Glen Rice!" Rice's sons were also competitive, and would flip a coin over who got to play as dad. When his kids began monopolizing the *NBA Jam* cabinet, Rice went out and bought another one. "I never lost," he said with a laugh. "I didn't take it easy on the kids either."

Elsewhere in Florida, Shaquille O'Neal was playing the game, too. After the Orlando Magic star saw *NBA Jam* in the arcade, he told his agent to contact the people who made the game to get him one as quickly as possible. In college, Shaq got into basketball video games by playing *Double Dribble*, but when *Jam* arrived, everything else was left in the dust. "The game gave us superpowers," Shaq told me. "The graphics were a good part of the game, but the guy with the voice—he made it."

When Shaq got his *NBA Jam* cabinet, it went right into his game room, right by his *Terminator 2* cabinet. Anfernee "Penny" Hardaway and Dennis Scott, his teammates on the Magic, lived nearby and would come over to Shaq's place for *NBA Jam* matches. According to Shaq, he and Scott were once playing in front of a large group when Shaq went on a tear and hit an astounding twelve three-pointers in a row, including one from half-court. That was when things got heated.

Unlike Rice, Shaq never played as himself in *NBA Jam*. "In real life, I always wanted to be that player that could step out and shoot the three when needed, and that wasn't really my game," Shaq said. "I wasn't concerned with flipping and dunking and all that. I was concerned with doing stuff that I couldn't do in real life." As a result, he always chose the Indiana Pacers to play as Reggie Miller or the Golden State Warriors for Mullin. "I would always go to the corner and hit that three, and used to love to get to that point," Shaq said, pausing to do his best Tim Kitzrow impression. "HE'S ON FIRE!"

•

Tzk-heet, tzk-heet, tzk-heet

In fall 1993, the laser printer at the University of Kentucky computer lab cranked its familiar rhythms again. Once more, Randolph Vance stood close, ready to pick up and staple the printed pages. But in this instance, the paper in his hands wasn't their guide, and when he and Greg Henderson left the lab, their destination wasn't the Kentucky Arcade.

After their many conversations with Turmell, Vance and Henderson got curious about the Midway office, so they gently asked if they could visit. Turmell gave them the go-ahead, so Vance and Henderson got their friend Chris to drive them over to Chicago in his Honda. Over a long weekend in November, the friends headed out of Lexington onto Interstate 65. Six hours later, they made it to 3401 North California Avenue.

Arriving late that night, Vance and Henderson were surprised to find that Midway wasn't headquartered in the best part of town. From the outside, the complex looked quaint and low-tech, like some kind of 1950s widget factory.

But as soon as the friends made it in, they could tell that this was where the hottest arcade games were made. Turmell was still in the office, hanging out with other developers. He took Vance and Henderson on a tour of the factory, and the friends from Lexington got to know this once-mysterious figure in person. Turmell had a whimsical Willy Wonka-like quality to him, Vance thought, but he was a relatable computer geek, too.

Turmell introduced the friends to his coworkers, including Sal DiVita. The group talked about games for a bit, then headed to play some. Vance and Henderson sampled the *Star Trek: The Next Generation* pinball table a few months before its release. Because the game was unfinished, they were warned to avoid certain targets since the code wasn't fixed or else they might crash the game. As they roamed between rooms, the excess of cans, coffee cups, and clutter made one thing clear: This was not just a workplace but a sort of second home for the developers who worked here.

Vance and Henderson had also brought a gift of sorts for Turmell. One of them handed Turmell a stack of printed paper—around 50 pages of ideas and improvements for the next *NBA Jam* game, all supplied by their Usenet community at rec.video. games.arcade. The suggestions included adding an internal clock to trigger timely messages, ad spaces that could be customized to feature local businesses, and a special "tournament mode" that disabled certain features so arcade operators could run serious *NBA Jam* tournaments. Turmell leafed through the pages and thanked them, impressed by the material.

On this occasion, Turmell had another secret to share. He pointed them in the direction of the arcade where *NBA Jam* had first appeared in case they wanted to play some games while they were in Chicago. Sure enough, when Vance and Henderson walked into Dennis' Place for Games later that weekend, none other than Willie "Air" Morris Jr. was there holding court on a brand-new *Mortal Kombat II* machine. Morris was dominating the machine, beating opponent after opponent on just two quarters, and Vance and Henderson joined the line of challengers. The starstruck friends met and played one of *NBA Jam*'s greatest secret characters and the man whose moves defined the game. Then, Air Morris turned them into casualties number 51 and 52. Losing at a game had never been so exhilarating.

The trip to Chicago made the perfect cap to 1993, Vance and Henderson's year of *NBA Jam*. Even the Holiday Inn where they stayed had an *NBA Jam* near the vending machines. "It was a pretty good year, I tell you what," Vance recalled to me. "It was a really interesting year."

The broader impact of the game rippled across Midway. The Amusement & Music Operators Association named *NBA Jam* "Most Played Video Game for 1993," and the *Chicago Tribune* wrote, in January 1994, that it "has become the highest earner in the industry's history despite being on the market just eleven months."

As Midway fulfilled order after order, *NBA Jam* machines traveled across the world. John Carlton found one while on vacation in Bologna, Italy. When he and his wife walked past an arcade, Carlton popped his head in out of curiosity, only to see *NBA Jam* and a big crowd surrounding it. *Jam* cheerleader Lorraine Olivia bumped into another on her honeymoon in Jamaica.

In Chicago, Tim Kitzrow found his own ways to enjoy the game's popularity. On occasion, he would visit an arcade, find the nearest *NBA Jam*, and spontaneously yell "BOOMSHAKALAKA!" or "HE'S ON FIRE!" behind players on the machine. Players would turn around and tell him, "You sound a lot like the guy from the game." Another time, he played ball with kids at a YMCA and called out each of their names in his *NBA Jam* voice.

Kitzrow got a surprise of his own in early 1994 when he was back at Williams Bally/Midway for another pinball gig. He stopped by the cafeteria for a bite when someone pointed him toward an article about *NBA Jam* that had been posted on a board. "Can you believe that the game took in a billion dollars?" he said. Kitzrow thought the guy was kidding, but then he got close to the text.

It was true. 250 million instances of fingers slipping coins into slots. 1,562-and-a-half tons of nickel-copper alloy. Four *billion* quarters. One *billion* dollars. And this was just for the arcade game.

Slowly, it sunk in. *NBA Jam* had earned ten digits for the arcade owners who put the machines on their floors, and here he—an integral part of the *Jam* experience—had made roughly a thousand dollars. "I was floored," Kitzrow recalled to me. "It was the first time I realized I was in a business and it wasn't just a fun hobby where my friends worked. It was the beginning of a long lifetime of fighting for appropriate compensation."

NBA Jam was a monster hit—even bigger than *Mortal Kombat*. Based on Turmell and DiVita's estimates, Midway sold 23,000 *NBA Jam* cabinets. They also sold 4,000 *Jam* "kits," which were reduced-price packages containing the guts of the game (such as its hardware and art) so an existing cabinet could be converted into *Jam*.

At Midway, the good news kept on coming. *Mortal Kombat II* was another juggernaut, topping *NBA Jam*'s astonishing sales. George Petro and Jack Haeger brought rock icons Aerosmith in for *Revolution X*, a shooting game set in a dystopia where music has been banned by an authoritarian regime. *NBA Jam* cheerleader Kerri Hoskins played the regime's militaristic leader Mistress Helga and soon quit her job at *Playboy* for one in video games. Eugene Jarvis had another hit with *Cruis'n USA*, one of the first arcade racers to link multiple cabinets.

There was more to come for *NBA Jam*, of course. In addition to Acclaim Entertainment getting to work on the home versions, Turmell and a revamped version of the *NBA Jam* development team worked on expanding and updating the coin-op version. *NBA Jam: Tournament Edition* (named as such because it added the kind of tournament mode Randolph Vance hoped for) piled on the features: updated rosters, half-time substitutions, more than two players selectable per team, more attributes per player, more moves, more calls, and refined gameplay.

When *Tournament Edition* arrived in arcades in 1994, it proved to be another unqualified success, selling loads more units and cementing *NBA Jam*'s reputation as a must-play game. *Tournament Edition* included a new "special thanks" screen in its attract mode, too. The names on the screen included Randolph Vance, William Henderson, and "many Internet users."

Mark Turmell's career had never been in a better place. Because the game sold such high numbers, he tapped into a rare and seemingly unattainable royalties bracket clause at Midway. He made seven figures on *NBA Jam*.

He had also been dating someone seriously. The two met in California, and when Turmell left for Illinois, he brought her with him. When the couple got married, they moved from a swanky condo to a regal 6,700-square-foot home in the suburbs, where they raised a daughter together. Turmell turned his walkout basement into an arcade packed with pinball tables and video game cabinets. Everyone called the home "the house that *NBA Jam* built."

CHAPTER 7:
"RAZZLE DAZZLE"

ON ITS SURFACE, *NBA Jam* was a small game. You moved back and forth on a tight playfield, always playing the same kind of game on the same court for the same crowd. There was nothing to customize, no supplemental modes or bonus features of any sort. Four players. One ball. That's it.

But as soon as gamers started digging, *NBA Jam*, *NBA Jam: Tournament Edition*, and the two games' many console adaptations revealed much, much more. Over the 1990s, *NBA Jam*'s lore grew to be filled with strange codes and peculiar stories, imbuing it with the same mystique the *Mortal Kombat* games had. No matter how far-fetched a rumor about *NBA Jam* was, it felt like there was a chance it was true. This aura went a long way in keeping the game on players' minds as new games arose to compete for *Jam*'s attention. In the case of the game's most famous hidden element—its secret characters—the whole thing started as a joke.

After wrapping up the game and admiring how well *NBA Jam* had turned out, someone on the development team suggested that they all get their faces digitized for the game. With the face-swapping system, substituting heads was easy to do, so why not put themselves in the game? It would make a fun little memento. One by one, each of the seven went up against the blue screen to have his image captured.

When it was Sal DiVita's turn in front of the blue screen, he stood stoically.

"All right, smile if you want," a voice behind the camera said.

"I don't want to smile," DiVita responded.

"Not even for the selection thing?" the cameraman said.

DiVita stayed silent. Locking in his most intimidating game face, he slowly rotated against the screen. He turned 360 degrees, allowing the camera to get a complete view of his features, including his long black mullet—the kind of haircut popular among the pro wrestlers of the era. Capturing DiVita took ten seconds. Then, it was on to the next developer.

Jon Hey stuck out his tongue. John Carlton dangled a cigarette out of his mouth. Shawn Liptak widened his eyes and jumped around. One by one, each of them stepped in front of the camera.

The developers buried themselves in *NBA Jam* through codes corresponding to their initials and birthdays that could entered at the start of a game. DiVita was SAL, February 1; Hey was JWH, September

20; Carlton was JMC, August 5; and so on. They quickly added their friends at Midway, and the blue screen actors, too. Everyone's heights and abilities were blown out of proportion, but hey, this was their game.

To the team's surprise, this in-joke proved to be of immense interest. Players everywhere compared notes about these unfamiliar characters and their skill sets. Lists of codes containing secret characters were taped to the sides of cabinets, and guides like "How to WIN at *NBA JAM*!" traveled far and wide outside Kentucky. One Midway distribution partner sent management an irate letter about the codes because of the frenzy they were causing. "Your programmers have created a monster," Lieberman Music Company president Stephen E. Lieberman wrote, attaching Vance and Henderson's FAQ, which was being sold to players in a Minneapolis arcade for $10 to $25 a copy. "I think that programmer creative freedom has gone too far."

Yet as *NBA Jam*'s earnings started to fade, rumors and codes were crucial to boosting them up. "Turmell and those guys were masters at spoon-feeding information to the press and the public at regular intervals," *Video Games & Computer Entertainment* editor Chris Bieniek said to me. "Eventually, they realized that it was actually easier—and even more effective, in the long term—to just straight-up lie about secret stuff because people would still keep trying different button combinations and guessing at the supposed hidden characters' initials and birthdates, hoping to be the first to discover a new secret." Vance and Henderson weren't the only sleuths who tracked down Mark Turmell's home number. One kid called and spoke to Turmell's wife, pretending to give a survey, just so he could get her initials and birthday to check if she was in *NBA Jam*. (She wasn't.)

Cheerleader codes became the most buzzed-about subject among *NBA Jam* fans. The cover of the August '93 issue of *VG&CE* boasted a screenshot of a digitized Kerri Hoskins coming in for a monster jam, implying that she (and, by proxy, Lorraine Olivia) *had* to be in the game somewhere. Players did everything they could to find them, testing combination after combination. The discussion began on message boards then led to players hunting down *Playboy* back issues for her initials and birthday. Some resourceful boys called *Playboy* directly, hoping to speak to the ladies themselves. As it so happened, the original screenshot was just a mock-up so *VG&CE* would have something cool for the cover, and the cheerleaders were never actually playable characters. When *Tournament Edition* came out, Hoskins and Olivia finally made it into the game, but not without Turmell hinting that they had been hidden in *NBA Jam* the entire time.

Because of his role as a secret character, John Carlton experienced one of the strangest moments of his life. The artist was at his desk one day when he heard a voice say, "Hey, it's Carlton." When he turned around, Macaulay Culkin was pointing at him. Three years after reaching superstar status with *Home Alone* and becoming one of the most famous people in the world, Culkin was in Chicago filming *Richie Rich* and had stopped by Midway for a tour. "I always play your secret character in *NBA Jam*," Culkin said to Carlton. Then he walked away.

With *Tournament Edition*, the roster of special guests ballooned. The Midway guys rented Halloween masks and invented a new batch of weirdos, like the Grim Reaper and a gorilla in a Viking helmet called Kongo. This time, nearly everyone who worked in video games at Williams Bally/Midway made it in. Eugene Jarvis showed up for his portrait in a straitjacket, cackling, with an X carved into his forehead. Ed Boon glared. John Tobias grinned. Including everyone in *NBA Jam* epitomized the high morale and team spirit of the era. Eric Kinkead, who did art and testing for *Tournament Edition*, once described the move to include everybody as "the point of Camelot for Midway, the round table and the white castle on the hill."

When Acclaim created the home versions of *NBA Jam*, secret characters took on an even more pronounced role. Acclaim first asked to add its own developers, which Midway agreed to, then had the idea to toss in celebrities. Instead of using digitization, the lower-resolution heads for the home games would be hand-drawn, allowing them to make anyone they imagined. The new draft of special guests included President Bill Clinton, Vice President Al Gore, Houston Oilers quarterback Warren Moon, and George Clinton, the man whose music inspired the game's soundtrack.

"I've seen it a couple of times and heard my hair caught on fire," George Clinton, who appeared in the game as "P-Funk," recalled to me. The legendary funk front man was in a bad place in the early 90s when *NBA Jam* came out ("At that time, I was a crackhead," he said), but he did hear from his grandkids that he was tearing up the hardwood. Clinton loved golden age arcade classics like *Pac-Man* and *Galaxian*, but he never played *Jam*. "I never could get the coordination when games started controlling people running up and down the court," he said. "In *Galaga*, I got that, but when it came to real-life shit, I couldn't even do that on Nintendo."

Rumors about who else might be in the game grew increasingly bizarre. According to reports, musicians Ted Nugent and Red Hot Chili Peppers bassist Flea appeared in prototypes of the home game. *GamePro* editor Dan Amrich dedicated a portion of his online *NBA Jam* guide to clarifying who was *not* in the game. Contrary to gossip, the game did not contain Magic Johnson, Oprah Winfrey, Rush Limbaugh, Beavis & Butt-Head, Charles Manson, Darth Vader, Barney the Dinosaur, Al Pacino, or Michael Jackson. One gullible soul even wrote to Amrich asking whether or not Jackson really performed a halftime show.

By the time Acclaim plotted the home versions of *Tournament Edition*, an unpredictable roster of secret characters had become one of *NBA Jam*'s unspoken selling points, so the company pushed the concept further and further. With each new release, another outlandish name was in NBA Jam. You could hit the court as Hillary Clinton or Prince Charles, the Beastie Boys or Sonic Youth, Larry Bird or Heavy D, Chicago White Sox heavy hitter Frank Thomas or Philadelphia Eagles quarterback Randall Cunningham, the Fresh Prince of Bel-Air or DJ Jazzy Jeff.

"Yo, dude," someone said to DJ Jazzy Jeff, gesturing toward the television. "You're a character in the game." The DJ born Jeffrey Allen Townes was hanging out with friends when a group had fired up a game of *NBA Jam* and entered his code. In the 90s, Townes and Will Smith were hip-hop musicians as well as stars of a popular sitcom, plus they worked with the NBA on its "Stay in School" campaign, so they made an excellent fit for the game. It's likely that Smith played as himself in *NBA Jam*, according to Townes, though he typically didn't have the patience for video games.

Townes, on the other hand, was a serious gamer, having waited in line for *Jam* at the arcade even when he preferred simulation-style basketball games. He was dazzled by the cameo. Being a secret character in *NBA Jam* was, in his words, "almost a badge of honor." "Every musician I know wants to be a superstar in sports and every superstar in sports wants to be a musician. That's why you have so many rappers playing in celebrity basketball games," he said to me. "Every time you saw someone jump up and dunk with that character, that was actually me. *I* did that."

Little information is available on Acclaim's licensing and compensation for use of the special guests. The fine print on one of the game's boxes showed a copyright notice for George Clinton's "P-Funk" nickname, but Clinton did not recall ever receiving any payment or signing any agreement for his likeness. The same went for Townes. While Clinton thought his inclusion as a secret character was cool, he associated it with a time when he routinely went unpaid for use of his likeness and music. His career, he said, had been plagued by stories of reneged contracts and missing royalties. "*NBA Jam,*" he said, "is just one of 1,300 of them."

For Townes, memories were fonder. "The licensing agreement would have gone to the record company. Even if it was something handled correctly, it probably wouldn't have benefited any of the artists in the first place," he said. If a similar opportunity to be in another *NBA Jam* arose, Townes emphasized that he would say yes in a heartbeat, regardless of whether the money was good or bad or even if there was no money at all. "You don't realize how iconic something could be and what it could mean to someone. Sometimes, money gets in the way of that. I'm sure there were circumstances where money stopped history from being made in one shape or another. To me, it's the coolest shit in the world to tell my son that I was in a video game," Townes said. "I would be 100 percent in."

Beyond the Enter Your Initials menu, players could input codes on the Tonight's Matchup screen before a game started. As the game briefly displayed headshots of the competing teams, you could enter button and joystick combinations to alter how the game played. Tapping the Steal/Block button eight times boosted your defensive stats. Pressing it 21 times increased your offense. Hitting Up, Turbo, and Steal unlocked something particularly entertaining: Big Head Mode.

The time Tony Goskie had spent working on the player heads was well worth it, but *NBA Jam* moved so fast you barely got a chance to admire his work. Someone on the team suggested inflating the heads to make the details easier to see. Putting big heads on regular-sized bodies created a cartoony bobblehead-style look that some team members loved, enough to the point that Turmell floated it as being the default look for the players. Sal DiVita, for one, thought the visual was way too distracting.

As a compromise, Big Head Mode was incorporated into the game as a secret code. It proved to be a major hit among players and soon other developers were using the idea in other games such as *GoldenEye 007* and *Tony Hawk's Pro Skater*. To *VG&CE* editor Chris Bieniek, it represented something new. "It didn't make the game easier. It didn't allow you to skip anything. All it did was make you laugh and make the game look different," he said. "That's a really powerful thing, from a word-of-mouth perspective: a cheat code that doesn't 'ruin' the game but actually makes it more interesting and fun."

An even crazier treasure was buried in the Tonight's Matchup screen: a whole other game. If Player 1 and Player 2 held all their buttons and Down, Player 1 would be transported to the "Tank Game." In its trippy early 3D landscape, you fired at enemy vehicles and navigated among polygons. The Tank Game was difficult, but if you survived, you turned on power-ups for all players, juicing *NBA Jam* to the gills.

Programmer Shawn Liptak made the Tank Game as a tech demo for an idea he had for a game inspired by Atari's arcade classic *Battlezone*. Impressively, he figured out how to make Midway's 2D-oriented hardware draw 3D graphics, so he snuck the game into *NBA Jam* on a lark. If someone knew it existed, they might spend a few extra quarters trying it out, he figured.

But as it turned out, the code wasn't the only way to access the Tank Game. DiVita was in Turmell's office fiddling around on a *Jam* cabinet when he pulled off the code in the game's attract mode. Turmell noticed what happened and was startled. "Did you coin in?" he asked. DiVita hadn't, and Turmell freaked out. This had the makings of a disaster. Players could potentially hog *NBA Jam* to play the Tank Game without spending a cent.

Due to a programming oversight, it turned out that the Tank Game was indeed always accessible in the attract mode. Getting flashbacks of arcade owners upset over the Pleasure Domes in *Smash T.V.*, Midway frantically burned and shipped out new glitch-free boards, and asked video game magazines to avoid spreading the secret in their pages.

The kerfuffle ended up being a whole lot of nothing. Performing the code took knowledge and work, and no one was going to waste precious minutes on *NBA Jam* for a game so simple and a secret so obscure. Had anything come of it, the Tank Game might have qualified as Midway's first 3D game, but the project never made it off the ground, leaving its appearance in *NBA Jam* as its only trace.

Another glitch spooked the team in a different way. Turmell and his coworkers were playing *Mortal Kombat II* at the office when, on the *NBA Jam* machine next to them, Tim Kitzrow's voice burst out of nowhere, saying "PETROVIĆ!" The bug only happened with this one name and at random, but it happened again and again.

In the early 90s, Dražen Petrović emerged as one of the NBA's most promising players. An aggressive and creative shooter, the Croatian-born Petrović was a rising star on the New Jersey Nets in an era when European players were rare. Then, on June 7, 1993, Petrović was on an autobahn in Germany when a semi-truck slammed into the car he was riding in and killed him, three months before he turned 29. Petrović's sudden death cast a shadow in the NBA, and the Nets retired his jersey later that year, but his image remained fresh because he appeared alongside Derrick Coleman on the Nets in *NBA Jam*. After his passing, Midway staffers started witnessing the glitch.

Late one night, Jon Hey was walking through the darkened factory when "PETROVIĆ!" burst right out of a machine. Hey got the shock of his life, and the ghost story grew. "It was absolutely true," Hey emphasized to me. "We all encountered it."

Kitzrow and Hey were both involved in another odd *NBA Jam* episode. After spending hours recording all the names and phrases for the original *NBA Jam* voiceover sessions, they decided to play around. *Jam* had all the essentials, and Kitzrow had done such a good job that they both wanted to hear his voice say more absurd things, like curse words. Kitzrow gamely let loose. "No fucking way!" "He's fucking up!" "Get that shit out of here!" The tape kept running and the two kept improvising, all in good fun.

Twenty years later, the classic gaming fan site Nintendo Player received an anonymous package. Inside was a green Super Nintendo circuit board marked *Jam XXX*. When played, the game turned out to be a version of *NBA Jam* containing those lost recordings. Instead of "Grabs the rebound!," Kitzrow would say, "Grabs his johnson!" Instead of "HE'S ON FIRE!," he would say, "HE'S ON FUCKING FIRE!" The effect allowed gamers to see a beloved old game through a warped kaleidoscope. The website published video of the game in action, and sure enough, the familiar voice in *NBA Jam XXX* sounded exactly like Tim Kitzrow.

But when gaming news website Kotaku asked Kitzrow for comment, he denied its legitimacy, chalking it up to "the YouTube hacks." "I'm still friends with a lot of those folks from Acclaim and Iguana," Kitzrow said, referencing the companies behind the home ports, "and no one knows who is pulling your chain. A good imitation to be sure, but trust me, *Jam* was too big to have ever messed around like that."

As it happens, those clips were the real Kitzrow after all. As an actor who generally keeps his comedy clean, he was initially concerned that the revelation of this joke would hurt his relationship with the NBA, but he has since grown more comfortable discussing those hijinks in the booth. "We spent a long time in there and it was like being on the playground," he told me, recalling that he recorded gag lines for Iguana, too. "People love to hear me use my voice for any variety of things. It was supposed to be a little in-joke between some people who worked on it."

Of course, there were never plans to actually use the material. Hey's theory is that a drive or disc containing the original sessions was sent over to Acclaim or Iguana as reference material for the home ports, and the phrases were buried in a folder until someone found them. The developer must have copied the audio and added it to a version of *NBA Jam* later or passed it on to someone who did. But another mystery remains unsolved: Who unearthed the audio and made *NBA Jam XXX* in the first place?

The NBA did learn about another bit of fun Midway had—and it was not pleased. At the time, *Mortal*

Kombat and *NBA Jam* were closely linked. The teams shared technology, space, talent, and knowledge. Tony Goskie went from making the court in *NBA Jam* to designing stages for *Mortal Kombat II*. After getting her start as a cheerleader in *Jam*, Kerri Hoskins's role as Sonya Blade in *Mortal Kombat 3* launched her into a new career. *Jam* and *MK* share the same point of origin, too. If *Total Carnage* hadn't fizzled, and Turmell and John Tobias had not decided to go their separate ways creatively, neither *NBA Jam* nor *Mortal Kombat* would exist as we know them.

This bond shined brightest in an early release of *NBA Jam: Tournament Edition*. In addition to the *Mortal Kombat* ads running along the sidelines and the *MK* developers appearing as special guests, *Tournament Edition* housed *MK* secret characters. Colorful models of Scorpion, Sub-Zero, Reptile, and Raiden went up and down with killer jams.

But as soon as the NBA found out that Midway hid characters from the most violent video game on the market into a product that had the league's name on it, they wanted them removed immediately, as well as some of the other secret characters, so out went the *MK* special guests in the next revision. If the NBA was upset with that move, they would have hated what else Turmell snuck in.

Using an elaborate button combo and particular in-game circumstances, you could enable Fatalities. In the *MK* world, Fatalities were brutal character-specific finishing moves critical to the game's popularity. In *NBA Jam*, they amounted to one relatively tame move. If the sequence was performed correctly, you could push your opponent hard enough to temporarily turn his body into flames—a play on how Scorpion spat fire at his victims in *MK*. The visual barely lasted a second and the boards containing the Fatality weren't out there for long, but the mere fact that a finishing move existed in *NBA Jam* gave players another subject for speculation.

Rumors of Michael Jordan appearing in *Jam* were common, too. As the biggest NBA player on the 90s, Jordan's absence was conspicuous. In a way, he had been with *Jam* since the beginning, with Willie Morris Jr. playing him in that pitch video, but as the final roster came together, keeping him proved to be impossible. Jordan had opted out of the NBA Players licensing agreement, meaning that his likeness was off the table for projects like this—unless Midway or Acclaim wanted to pay an exorbitant sum. Similar circumstances occurred with Shaquille O'Neal and Charles Barkley as they left *NBA Jam* and appeared in their own games.

Randolph Vance and William Henderson explained Jordan's whereabouts in a special note in their FAQ, but talk persisted. In July 1993, one user on rec.games. video.arcade breathlessly posted, "I just came back from the Mall of America, and there IS a Michael Jordan in the *NBA Jam* game!" Vance responded, "To which I say, 'SHEYYAH! RIIIIGHT!!!! Tell us ANOTHER ONE!'"

Yet because *NBA Jam* became such a craze, Michael Jordan himself later asked to be put into the game. Jordan's camp got in touch with Midway, asking the company to make a special version of *Jam* in which he was a playable character, just for his personal use. The team was happy to put him in the game and sent over a game with a unique EPROM chip.

Midway would do the same for Jordan's friends Gary Payton and Ken Griffey Jr. As part of the Seattle SuperSonics with Shawn Kemp, Payton would become a memorable presence in *NBA Jam: Tournament Edition*, but *NBA Jam* had left him out of the original roster, and he wanted that rectified. Griffey, the superstar slugger from the Seattle Mariners, was a massive *Jam* fan, too, so he had his head photographed from the requisite angles and sent the results over.

Today, the Jordan EPROMs exist in only two confirmed locations: mint-condition *NBA Jam* cabinets in Payton's garage, and somewhere among a pile of loose, unmarked boards stored in Turmell's house. The world has yet to see any evidence of Jordan in *NBA Jam* proper, but Turmell has teased that perhaps someday he'll dig the board out of storage and figure out a way to release it online. Until then, the Michael Jordan editions remain *NBA Jam*'s greatest mystery and a major source of interest among fans.

Even without Jordan, the Chicago Bulls were one of the best and most popular squads in the game, in and outside of the city. But Turmell felt sick at the thought of the Bulls being better than the Detroit Pistons in his own game. As development on *NBA Jam* was finishing, Turmell adjusted some code to level the playing field. If the Bulls were playing the Pistons and made a last-second rally, Scottie Pippen's stats would plummet, and the team's shots would average out to be bricks—a stark contrast to what happened in real life. With this change, Turmell made the prophecy from that text box in *Total Carnage* come true: "The Bulls win now, but the Pistons will rule the NBA again."

If all this wasn't enough to seal the win for Detroit, you could swap out Isiah Thomas or Bill Laimbeer for a Michigan native who was the single best *NBA Jam* character of them all. All you had to do was enter MJT, March 22. "Digitally, I'm tall, I'm as fast as Spud Webb, and I can shoot as good as Pippen," Mark Turmell said in a 1994 *Slam* magazine interview. Armed with a 9 out of 10 or 10 out of 10 in every statistical category, Turmell lived out his basketball fantasies with *NBA Jam*. "Kids recognize me, which is real funny. I sign some autographs now and then," he added. "I always thought that seeing your game on the shelves of Toys 'R' Us was a real kick, but to actually go out in arcades and see someone playing your head, that's even better."

CHAPTER 8:
"JAMS IT IN"

WHEN IT COMES TO RAGS-TO-RICHES rap songs, no light shines brighter than "Juicy" by The Notorious B.I.G. "It was all a dream," the Brooklyn rapper begins. As a funky, understated bass riff struts, Biggie unravels his life story of growing up hungry and poor, fantasizing about hip-hop glory, and achieving it all. Released in 1994, "Juicy" finds him peering over his riches: sold-out shows, a flush bank account, several homes, all the liquor and weed he could ever want, a mink coat for his mom, and diamond earrings for his baby girl. He has a 50-inch TV, too, and raps, "Super Nintendo, Sega Genesis / When I was dead broke, man, I couldn't picture this." In a song about achieving luxury, owning both of the hottest game systems at the same time exemplified the good life.

Most gamers in the early 90s didn't have the luxury of buying both systems, which set the stage for the 16-bit console wars between Nintendo and Sega. Both companies began their journeys in the video game business in the arcade, and when Atari went into decline, Nintendo seized the home market with Sega soon hot on its tail. In short order, the two became bitter rivals.

As the sequel to the mega-hit Nintendo Entertainment System (NES), the Super Nintendo Entertainment System (or Super Nintendo) exuded an air of tradition, familiarity, and reliability. Meanwhile, Sega pitched the Genesis as the cooler, more high-tech, and more adult alternative to its competitor's family-friendly product. "Genesis does what Nintendon't," snarled one ad campaign. Each system had a deep library of high-quality exclusive titles. Thankfully, *NBA Jam* was headed to both.

Before the game ever made it into arcades, its home licensing rights had already been spoken for by Acclaim Entertainment, Inc. Founded in 1987 by Greg Fischbach, Rob Holmes, and James Scoroposki, Acclaim started life as a toy company. Unlike Midway, which developed games from scratch, Acclaim was a publisher that bought games made by small studios, then packaged, marketed, and released the results. With 1986's *Star Voyager*, it became one of the first independent American companies to publish software for the NES. Its strategy concentrated on translating existing properties into games. The company snapped up licenses like Rambo, *The Simpsons*, and the World Wrestling Federation, as well as the American rights to certain Japanese games. It had even released its own NBA home game, *NBA All-Star Challenge* in late 1992. Acclaim quickly set up one of the biggest sales markets of any of Nintendo's third parties and built business interests in Asia and Europe, creating a seriously valuable portfolio. "The name on the box said a lot," Greg Fischbach, Acclaim's longtime CEO and co-chairman, said to me. "Then, we started looking at arcades."

In 1993, home games yielded revenues of $6.5 billion. By comparison, coin-op games made revenues of $8 billion. Sophisticated products by powerhouses such as Midway, Capcom, Konami, Namco, SNK, and Sega represented the best of the business. The elusive objective of any home port was for it to be "arcade-perfect." Making a port just like the original wasn't realistic given the hardware limitations of the 16-bit systems, but Acclaim had a good grasp on how to make its adaptations prosper anyway.

The Midway/Acclaim partnership began around 1990 when Fischbach met Neil Nicastro in Oyster Bay, New York, the city where Acclaim had its headquarters and the Nicastro family had a home. Since Midway had no reliable distribution partner or channel for home products, the two companies brokered a deal that granted Acclaim the right of first refusal on console versions of all Midway games through 1995. Acclaim took full advantage of the deal, releasing ports of games like *Narc* on the Nintendo and *Smash T.V.* on the Super Nintendo.

Acclaim's greatest asset was its vision for how big a game could be, which far exceeded Midway's. When Acclaim saw just how huge *Mortal Kombat* was in the arcades, it poured a whopping $10 million into marketing the home games. Print and TV commercials advertising "Mortal Monday"—its release day of September 13, 1993—went far and wide. In one famous TV spot, a kid yelled "MORTAL KOMBAT!" in the middle of a city street as people rushed in from all sides. Even Ed Boon was concerned Acclaim might be going overboard, but the campaign helped create a new form of nationwide *MK* hysteria. Within three weeks of Mortal Monday, Acclaim's *Mortal Kombat* had sold three million copies.

Excited by the phenomenal success of *NBA Jam* in arcades, Acclaim saw similarly extraordinary potential. To find the right development team to handle the home adaptations, Acclaim used a bidding process in which studios put in offers for contracts to take on the projects. Acclaim's objective was to make sure the games were translated as faithfully and efficiently as possible. Time was of the essence, as the company wanted to get the home versions onto shelves as quickly as possible so Acclaim could capitalize on the hype with another major campaign.

The right partner proved to be Iguana Entertainment. Based in Austin, Texas, Iguana was a well-oiled machine with the talent and infrastructure to deliver good games quickly. Over six months, the team in Austin and their colleagues in the United Kingdom took the game's code and assets from Midway, and developed versions for the Super Nintendo, Sega Genesis, and the portable Sega

Game Gear. Along the way, the Midway *Jam* team kept in touch with Iguana to answer questions and provide feedback.

"Back then, 8-bit games would take a year with a team of twelve people, but we were coming in at six or seven months on these games. We were on time. We had a really good relationship," Iguana project manager J. Moon recalled to me. "It was good and bad. They thought of us as their rainmaker. Because we were doing these games so fast, they expected it all the time."

Working under tight circumstances, Iguana dutifully remained faithful to the overall look and feel of the arcade game, even if its versions had to lose elements like the ultra-vivid colors and distinctive player heads. The Super Nintendo and Genesis ports had their differences—for one, the Super Nintendo got crisper graphics—but both were as fast and compulsively playable as Midway's original. Due to timing and licensing issues, rosters shifted around as well, with Nick Anderson taking Shaquille O'Neal's spot on the Orlando Magic.

The audio took the most noticeable hit. Due to memory restrictions on cartridges, Jon Hey's music was pared down or, in the event of the Super Nintendo version, removed entirely. Less room for calls also meant that Tim Kitzrow repeated himself with increasing frequency.

At one point, there was almost an even greater loss: Tim Kitzrow himself. Because he made such a small amount on the arcade game, which proved to be more successful than he ever imagined, Kitzrow hoped to make more doing voiceovers for the home games and asked for $3,000. Acclaim, however, insisted on paying him the same amount. Jon Hey encouraged Kitzrow to fight for his money as Acclaim was poised to make millions off *NBA Jam*. Kitzrow stayed firm at $3,000, but Acclaim wouldn't budge. After going back and forth, Kitzrow believed he had lost his role in *NBA Jam* and felt dumb about fighting for the money. Eventually, an audio producer at Acclaim convinced the company that Kitzrow *was* the voice of *NBA Jam* and should be paid accordingly, and Acclaim changed its mind. "It was nice that it worked," Kitzrow recalled. "I had always been so naïve. I thought any money was good money."

As Iguana finished developing the home games, Acclaim Entertainment put its marketing plans into motion. Licensing aside, Acclaim set its games apart from the pack by creating eye-catching ad campaigns. Designing and planning a campaign for an original game was difficult when development timelines changed so frequently, but adapting an arcade game was a relatively quick process, making them much safer bets. Acclaim decided to go all out with *NBA Jam* and do another $10 million campaign.

The hype started with a one-page ad published in comic books and game magazines. White text with the words "JAM JAM JAM JAM" in all capitals filled a black background. At the bottom was a date (March

'94), the names of three systems (Super Nintendo, Sega Genesis, and Game Gear), and the Acclaim insignia. The page didn't have any screenshots or illustrations, not even an NBA logo. It didn't matter. Everyone knew what was coming.

All roads led to Friday, March 4, 1994 or, as Acclaim dubbed it, "Jam Day." Acclaim printed up *NBA Jam* pins, pennants, and posters for promotions, then went for a full-fledged media blitz with an assortment of ads. Its centerpiece was a 45-second commercial shot in Los Angeles. The spot began with street ballers in different settings—behind a chain-link fence, on an asphalt court, outside a suburban home—staring daggers at the camera. They had just one word to say: "Jam." Between these visuals, a first-person perspective scanned an empty basketball arena as the console names flashed by. When the music crescendoed, your view jumped impossibly high into the air and then through the hoop itself. The ad burst into fast-forwarded clips of *NBA Jam* gameplay and real NBA footage, making the two synonymous. For something that would run on not just television but in theaters, too, the propulsive commercial was perfect.

"It played off the popularity and soul of basketball. It was more about hoops than the video game," Sam Goldberg, who ran Acclaim's marketing department and spearheaded both the *Jam* and *Mortal Kombat* campaigns, recalled to me. "You knew there was a market for *NBA Jam*. If you could replicate that experience at home, you were going to have a success. The problem was how big of a success it was going to be. If this game wasn't a blow-out, it was my fault."

Goldberg had nothing to worry about. *NBA Jam* became a hit all over again on consoles, selling a combined six million copies on the Sega Genesis and Super Nintendo. Just as Midway paid the NBA a fee for each *NBA Jam* cabinet it sold, Acclaim paid Midway a fee for each copy it sold based on the original.

Game magazines showered the adaptations with praise, and *NBA Jam* received more ink than ever. *GamePro* called the Genesis port "a first-rate ball bouncer, and one of the best hoops games out there," and the Game Gear conversion "a tasty treat that you can take with you." *Nintendo Power* described the Super Nintendo adaptation as "the supreme court multiplayer extravaganza." On its cover, *Electronic Gaming Monthly* asked, "Better than *Mortal Kombat*? Better than *Street Fighter 2*? *NBA Jam*: the hottest new home game of the year!"

Fans of the coin-op game, like Shaquille O'Neal, were fired up about playing *NBA Jam* in a new format. According to popular rumor, Shaq was such a fan that he owned two machines: one that stayed at home and another that traveled with the Orlando Magic from town to town. He has since refuted the story about the road-only cabinet ("That would have been too much," he said to me), but he did keep the *Jam* action going strong on the Sega Genesis.

In that period, it was common for Shaq to step off the bus in a new town and tell his teammates,

"Tournament in the room at ten o' clock. Be there or hear about it tomorrow." Members of the memorable 90s Magic squad—among others, Penny Hardaway, Dennis Scott, and Nick Anderson—gathered with Shaq in hotel rooms to face off on the console court and exchange thousands of dollars. "Instead of partying at night, we'd be in a room hanging out and playing *NBA Jam*, putting money in the pot, seeing who could beat who," Shaq remembered. "It was awesome."

The home versions also introduced the game to players who lived in places where the arcade version was never available, and players who never went to arcades in the first place. The Super Nintendo port was how John Romero, the game designer and Mark Turmell fan from the Apple II days, encountered *NBA Jam*. At a time when Romero and his studio id Software were sending shockwaves through the PC game market with the epic first-person shooter *Doom*, he found time for *Jam*. "I absolutely never played sports games, but that was the one sports game I played," Romero said. "The fact that the ball was on fire meant that it was more of an arcade-y game. That was more interesting to me than trying to play an actual sports game."

Acclaim brought *NBA Jam* to the Game Boy and the Sega CD, and the sales kept coming. Based partly on the success of its *Jam* adaptations, Acclaim bought Iguana Entertainment in December 1994 and converted it into Acclaim Studios Austin. Acclaim understood *NBA Jam*'s value as a brand and deeply enjoyed its fame, but even Acclaim wasn't expecting the kind of reaction that happened when the public met Air Dog.

When Eric Samulski was a kid, his dad had the coolest job in the world. As Licensing and Marketing Director at Acclaim, Paul Samulski had inside access to all the newest, most impressive video games. Sometimes, Paul would bring Eric to the office and let him playtest the games before release. Paul even found ways to sneak Eric into them, like naming a player in *Roger Clemens' MVP Baseball* after him or throwing him a special thanks on *Krusty's Super Fun House*. Eric never knew where he would show up next.

Paul also happened to be an avid photographer, which meant that Eric never paid much mind when his dad asked him for a photo. Once, Paul snapped a headshot of a 9-year-old Eric, who half-smiled for the camera, his front teeth missing.

The next thing Eric knew, Paul was showing him how to unlock himself in the home versions of *NBA Jam*. He was in the game under the alias "Air Dog," a play on "Er" (pronounced "air"), which was something Paul called him. "My dad just thought it was a better nickname than putting in my real name," Eric recalled to me. "It was never something I was called before."

Air Dog was the youngest and smallest player in *NBA Jam*, darting around the court and delivering huge jams. The novelty and excitement of having his own *Jam* character (especially in an era before create-a-player modes) was never lost on Eric. He always felt obligated to play as himself, even after he learned his character wasn't actually that good. For a few weeks, his cameo upped his social status among his friends. "Then," he said, "it got to the point where they couldn't wait to play me in *NBA Jam* and talk trash to me on multiple levels: one to me sitting next to them, one to me as a virtual character."

Around that time, Acclaim began running a booth at the annual NBA All-Star Weekend to showcase its latest *NBA Jam* games; the company revealed the first ports in Minneapolis in 1994. In 1996, Eric went with his dad to the All-Star Weekend in San Antonio, Texas. Eric was hanging out at Acclaim's booth when someone came up to him with a surprising question: "Are you Air Dog?"

Soon, another person noticed him, then another. Word quickly spread that there were other *NBA Jam* secret characters at the booth, too, like Acclaim staffers Asif Chaudhri and Eric Kuby. With a crowd gathering, the Acclaim team decided to have some fun and used a table for an impromptu autograph station. Someone handed Eric a marker. He could barely write his own name legibly and here he was about to inscribe programs, envelopes, and whatever else strangers put in front of him. "Should I sign as Eric or Air Dog?" he asked his dad, having never had to think about such a thing before. "Nobody knows the hell Eric Samulski is," Paul said. "They're talking to you because you're Air Dog." In his clearest script, Air Dog carefully signed his new name.

Eric had the thrill of his life that weekend. "It's one thing to be involved in a video game. It's another to have someone coming up and asking for your autograph, especially considering I was an athlete as a kid, and one of the quintessential athlete moments is signing autographs for people," he said to me. "Looking back on it, the visual of people asking a ten-year-old for an autograph is still hilarious."

Air Dog returned when Acclaim brought *NBA Jam: Tournament Edition* home in February 1995. With *Tournament Edition*'s ads and box art, Acclaim introduced a key image into *NBA Jam* lore: an airbrushed photo of a basketball literally on fire. These releases were massive sellers, too, racking up millions more in sales, and Acclaim ported the game to every platform it could. The *Jam* hysteria seemed like it would never end.

As *NBA Jam*'s reputation grew, Acclaim and Iguana's influence on the in-game product expanded beyond putting in secret characters to changing the gameplay itself. In home versions of *Tournament Edition*, players could not just do the trademark wild dunks but rocket to the hoop from the opposite side of the court as if they were roman candles. New hot spot modes added eight-point and nine-point shots, leading to absurd scores. These kinds of changes were too much for Turmell. To him, the charm of *NBA Jam* was in exaggerated reality, not outright wackiness.

It also became clear that *NBA Jam* was making more money for Acclaim than for Midway. "I mean, look at the revenue model," Greg Fischbach said, illustrating an example. "You sell 15,000 arcades at $2,000 apiece, and you sell two million units of a game at $40 apiece. Now, which one's more successful?"

Together, Midway and Acclaim were operating at the peak of their powers. The success of both companies proved that *NBA Jam* had all the makings of a franchise. What that future looked like would be shaped by only one of them.

CHAPTER 9:
"THE TURNOVER"

SOMETIME AROUND 1994, a spectre in purple and black appeared in Midway's blue screen studio. Standing at a formidable 6'10", he had pale skin, long hair, and ominous tattoos. His name was the Undertaker, he was here from the World Wrestling Federation, and he refused to work until someone got him a bottle of whiskey.

Riding the high of *NBA Jam*, Mark Turmell and most of his team jumped into another high-spectacle sports fantasy bolstered by a huge license. *WWF WrestleMania* starred eight of the biggest names in pro wrestling battling with an inventive blend of strikes, holds, and projectiles. For his signature Chokeslam move, the Undertaker would grab his opponent by the throat, shoot to the rafters, and slam him to the mat with the ferociousness of an *NBA Jam* dunk. He would hit you with his Tombstone Piledriver maneuver, then with a literal tombstone. Everyone else had similarly outrageous moves. Between the eye-popping colors, loud music, and out-of-control action, *WrestleMania* was pure Turmell.

When originally plotting the game, Mark Turmell expected to have to find stand-ins to play the wrestlers similar to how he found local athletes to stand in for the pros in *NBA Jam.* To his surprise, the World Wrestling Federation was happy to send the real talent straight to Midway's doorstep. The team hung out with wrestlers for hours and had a blast. Sal DiVita, in particular, enjoyed teaching the wrestlers how to execute their moves properly against the blue screen and using his body as a stunt dummy.

Outside the office, the developers and wrestlers got drunk at a bar near the arena in Chicago where the WWF ran shows. Making the whole project was a fantastic experience, and the game looked great and played well.

Then, it came time to put it on test. Unfortunately, the release of *WWF WrestleMania* in 1995 coincided with the hype for *Mortal Kombat 3* hitting a fever pitch. One time, the team visited an arcade to see how its game was doing and found a large crowd. They were gathered around *MK3*; *WrestleMania* was being used as a coat rack. "That game was one of our first realizations of, 'Oh, we don't know everything,'" DiVita reflected in a 2015 interview with Team GFB Radio. "Because we peaked so early, we thought anything we could make would be successful."

The problem with *WrestleMania* proved to be that it was not quite a fighting game and not quite a wrestling game. While *WrestleMania* didn't perform up to expectations in the arcade, the game found its audience at home through Acclaim's impressive home conversions, which retitled it to *WWF WrestleMania: The Arcade Game*. Of course, the project would never have been possible in the first place without Acclaim and its access to the WWF license. *WrestleMania* marked one of the final collaborations between Acclaim and Williams Bally/Midway as the days ticked on their contract.

The partnership had been prosperous beyond their wildest expectations thanks to Acclaim's marketing forte and Midway's skillful game design. But Midway had other ambitions.

In March 1994, talk swirled that Midway would cut ties with Acclaim and head into the lucrative home market on its own. "These rumors are unsubstantiated," an Acclaim spokeswoman told *Variety* magazine, but chatter was enough to hurt the company's stock since as much as 75 percent of Acclaim's revenue came from licensing Midway's products. The following month, Williams Bally/Midway acquired the Texas home game company Tradewest, which it swiftly rebranded to Midway Home Entertainment.

Ultimately, Midway and Acclaim decided to part ways. The biggest lingering question of their separation became who would get to make the next *NBA Jam*. Both companies had played a substantial role in building the

NBA Jam brand, which itself was owned by the league and had been licensed to Midway and Acclaim on a limited basis.

When the smoke cleared, the answer was a bombshell. In a press release, Acclaim announced that it had exclusive rights to the *NBA Jam* license. Midway would never touch *NBA Jam* again.

"We were all stunned," Turmell recalled. As the news coursed through the halls of Midway, anger and disbelief followed in its wake. Someone yelled, "I can't fucking believe it!" In Shawn Liptak's mind, whatever idiot allowed this to happen deserved to be fired. How could Midway lose one of its two biggest games just like that?

Parsing exactly what happened is tricky. The situation appears to have started when the contract was ending. A licensing director of the NBA's electronic toys and games department (who had previously worked at Acclaim) asked Midway about its plans for *NBA Jam*'s future. Midway said that it wanted to do something "new" and "innovative." The conversation was brief. There are multiple, competing stories about what happened next.

The account largely shared by the original *NBA Jam* team points to the NBA licensing director allegedly getting Midway to relinquish its ties to the *Jam* license under questionable circumstances. By saying things like "new" and "innovative" in that conversation, Midway was using the innocuous, generic language of a company uncertain of its next step. This did not mean that

Midway didn't have plans to return to *NBA Jam*. In fact, it learned about the change through a press release. "It was a very shady thing that happened," Sal DiVita said, preferring not to discuss the employee at the heart of the matter by name.

Frustration with Acclaim was seemingly already brewing at Midway. "We were never impressed with Acclaim's work," programmer Shawn Liptak recalled in a 2010 interview with 1Up.com. "They took our stuff, and slapped their name on it, and hacked up on it, and released it." In 1996, Iguana Entertainment developed and Acclaim released *College Slam*, a college-themed console game that was a carbon copy of *NBA Jam*. The game looked, played, sounded, and felt just like Iguana's hit *Jam* home ports with minimal changes. Instead of pro teams, you played as schools such as Duke University, Wake Forest University, the University of Kentucky, and the Ohio State University. Instead of being based on actual people, every *College Slam* player was identified by their position alone, with names like "CENTER," "SML FWD" ("Small Forward"), and "SHT GRD" ("Shooting Guard"). To Mark Turmell, *College Slam* felt like Acclaim pumping out a *Jam* knockoff. "They basically ruined the property," Turmell said. "They drove the two-on-two basketball mechanic into the ground with bad products and a bad reputation."

Speaking to the Acclaim employee-turned-NBA-licensing-director revealed a different perspective. He had fond memories of working on *NBA Jam* and said that there was never any deception involved. He also pointed out that while at the NBA, he maintained an excellent working relationship with Midway for years after the *Jam* license changed hands. "Midway, through their licensing group, told me specifically that they were not going to continue with the *NBA Jam* franchise. They were going to go in a different direction," the director told me. "Acclaim was very successful with the home versions and entering the arcade market as well, so the license was granted to them. That's as simple as I can put it."

Acclaim CEO Greg Fischbach asserted that the idea for *NBA Jam* came from Acclaim, so the company had a stake to the license from the start. (In contrast, Midway's Roger Sharpe said the original agreement for *NBA Jam* was a standalone deal for the arcade game.) Neither Fischbach nor the licensing director heard any complaints from Midway about this issue or sensed any animosity. Fischbach dismissed the notion of any tension between the companies, pointing out that the companies were close on an executive level—so close that they once considered merging. "Midway and ourselves had long conversations about putting the two companies together then at one point just decided that we couldn't make a deal, so we walked away from it," Fischbach said to me. "And we were fine. Everybody was happy."

Searching for the truth in the middle indicates that Midway did hope to do another *NBA Jam* but hesitated on making a decision until the last minute. By then, it was too late. Acclaim, on the other hand, was strongly committed to *NBA Jam*, and it planned to build *Jam* into a franchise, no questions asked.

By the mid-1990s, the console wars were shifting. New systems offered rapidly increasing processing power and graphical capabilities. Cartridges were being phased out for CDs, meaning that developers had loads more room for data to play with. Following a deal with Nintendo that went awry, Sony joined the fray with the 32-bit Sony PlayStation. On the system's launch day in September 1995, Acclaim released a high-quality port of *NBA Jam: Tournament Edition* for the PlayStation, as well as one for the 32-bit Sega Saturn. These versions re-added visual elements from the arcade game that past conversions removed, such as the vivid colors and distinct player heads. Aesthetics would not have to be sacrificed on home games much longer. Arcade-perfect was inches away.

The game industry had also latched onto the concept of 3D. In game design and marketing materials alike, three-dimensional games were heralded as the future. Compared to the speed at which the industry was moving and the possibilities polygons offered, digitization was becoming obsolete. Acclaim jumped at the chance to move *NBA Jam* from two dimensions to three. At its booth at the 1996 NBA All-Star Weekend in San Antonio, the company introduced *NBA Jam Extreme*.

Just as Midway had been making inroads to the home market, Acclaim began tinkering with coin-op. First, the company produced a *Batman Forever* game. Then, it had Iguana Entertainment, since renamed Acclaim Studios Austin, create an all-new 3D *NBA Jam* for arcades, using Washington Bullets forward Juwan Howard as its motion capture model.

Unfortunately, 3D technology was in its infancy, and *NBA Jam Extreme* lacked the finesse and care of past *Jam* games. It was cluttered with clunky models, glitchy animations, and muddy colors. You could barely recognize a face on the court. The camera swung constantly, making it difficult to keep up with the action. The newly added "Extreme" button served as an enhanced version of the Turbo button (which was also retained), but the update hardly qualified as a bonus. "I remember people thinking, 'It's going to be in 3D. Yeah!' and then being really disappointed in the actual gameplay," *GamePro*'s Dan Amrich recalled. "The Extreme button only served to overcomplicate the simple elegance of those three-button controls."

The game's signature voice was out as well. Although Tim Kitzrow had developed a consistent working relationship with Acclaim—Kitzrow voiced not just *College Slam* but other sports games like *Frank Thomas Big Hurt Baseball*, too—the company wanted someone else in *NBA Jam*. Acclaim offered Marv Albert—the very inspiration for Kitzrow's voice—a rumored six-figure deal to provide commentary for *NBA Jam Extreme*. But while Albert was a master at commentating actual NBA games, he was woefully out of his element in the arcade, especially having to follow Kitzrow's act. Albert lacked the over-the-top panache to draw in players, plus the material he had to work with wasn't nearly as strong. Instead of saying "He's heating up!," Albert delivered the weaker "I smell smoke!" When it came time to say "Boomshakalaka!," Albert's delivery was measured and skeptical, as if he was still practicing how to best deliver the line instead of recording the final, enthused take. Compared to Kitzrow, Albert was lethargic.

By all measures, *NBA Jam Extreme* tanked. Cabinet sales were, in Greg Fischbach's words, "horrible, horrible, horrible." Home sales were miserable, too, and critical reviews were low to middling. Reviewing the Sega Saturn version, Josh Smith of GameSpot wrote, "After spending an hour with this game, you'll probably feel the *Extreme* urge to *Jam* the Saturn through the television screen."

Extreme would be one of Acclaim's very few attempts at coin-op and the final *NBA Jam* game to appear in arcades. That misfire didn't deter the company from thinking big. Acclaim envisioned *NBA Jam* as a property that could sustain annual updates. Christmas 1998 yielded *NBA Jam '99*, a more realistic five-on-five simulation that was *Jam* in name alone. That three-dimensional game and its sequels *NBA Jam 2000*, *NBA Jam 2001*, and *NBA Jam 2002* showed the series becoming bloated and overexposed. Gaming magazines sidelined their coverage of *NBA Jam* from multi-page features to inconspicuous blurbs and sidebars.

Even after re-incorporating the two-on-two mode and making other adjustments, the sales just didn't materialize. The latest crop of NBA Jam games were neither great arcade-style sports games nor simulations. "Doing *NBA Jam* correctly would have been very profitable for the company, so therefore you continue to try and push it forward," Greg Fischbach said. "It wasn't Mark Turmell's vision by any stretch of the imagination."

In 2003, Acclaim took one more shot with a reimagining simply titled *NBA Jam*. This game reincorporated *Jam* trademarks like "on fire," hot spots, superhuman dunks, big heads, Tim Kitzrow's voice, and an absence of fouls, but instead of being two-on-two, the play was three-on-three. The game's most striking addition was a mode that allowed you to play basketball across different decades, such as the 1970s or 1980s, each with its own visual style, music, and commentary. Acclaim poured significant resources into the game, enlisting players from the trampoline basketball league SlamBall for motion capture and veteran funk bassist Bootsy Collins to do music and commentary.

But this game didn't garner much of a following either. Competition from other basketball games was fierce—Midway, Electronic Arts, Konami, Sony, Nintendo, Sega, and others had been battling in the space for years—and little from Acclaim's games truly stood out. Dan Amrich doesn't attribute *NBA Jam*'s fall in reputation to Acclaim's handling of the series as much as he does to time itself. "Like in any genre, the more sequels that arrive, the harder it is to sustain interest over a long period," he said. "Some things just have a natural moment in the sun, and when that sun sets, it's because something else is shining brighter."

As the years passed after its deal with Midway, Acclaim had found success with licensed games and franchises such as *Turok*, *Burnout*, and *NFL Quarterback Club*, but marketing and name recognition weren't enough to move enough units to create long-term sustainability. Internal strife was affecting the company, too.

Proud to scoff at controversy, Acclaim's marketing increasingly leaned into edginess and bad taste. *BMX XXX* took the framework of *Dave Mirra Freestyle BMX* and gave it an R-rated facelift involving topless strippers and profanity; Mirra later sued Acclaim to dissociate himself from the series. To promote *Burnout 2: Point of Impact*, Acclaim planned to cover British drivers' speeding tickets for one day; the UK government thought Acclaim was promoting reckless driving and the plan was dropped. For *Turok: Evolution*, the company offered to pay $10,000 to the first set of parents who named their baby after the game's hero. Most egregiously, for the UK release of *Shadow Man: 2econd Coming*, a game about exploring the underworld of death, Acclaim offered to pay relatives of the recently deceased to advertise the game by putting small billboards on the headstones. Payments would be calculated based on the exposure potential of a particular headstone, and Acclaim added that the offer might "particularly interest poorer families."

One morning in August 2004, Acclaim employees went to work at the company's headquarters in New York and found the doors padlocked shut. Effective immediately, it was filing for chapter 7 bankruptcy.

In 2006, Howard Marks, a former executive at Activision, picked up the company's name in bankruptcy court for just $100,000. He briefly revived Acclaim as an online game company. Then, in 2010, social media gaming company Playdom acquired Marks' Acclaim Games then permanently shuttered its servers shortly thereafter.

Unlike a music or movie company, Greg Fischbach found that a video game company had to refresh its catalog constantly as systems kept changing, and older products would generate little to no revenue. "What game companies do is recreate themselves every year," he said. "Have a couple of bad years in a row in terms of your products, and you find that you're at the end of the pier."

Acclaim would be far from the only casualty of the competitive churn of the game business, as company after company from the 90s would go out of business or be swallowed by someone else. Soon after its partnership with Acclaim ended, Midway had its own storms brewing.

CHAPTER 10:
"THE REBOUND"

"BETWEEN SEKTOR AND RAIDEN, who would win?" artist and actor Sal DiVita asked out loud before answering his own question: "Sektor's got—"

"Raiden would win," said Carlos Pesina.

DiVita turned to his side. He couldn't believe Pesina had interrupted him to say something so stupid. "Sektor's got it in the bag," DiVita fired back nonchalantly, but Pesina was insistent. "Raiden would win," he repeated, nudging DiVita's shoulder. DiVita retaliated by slapping the ballcap off Pesina's head. Pesina then jolted out of his chair and threw down a challenge. "We can settle this outside, man."

Each actor reached to his side and grabbed a piece of headgear conveniently located nearby. Putting on Raiden's conical hat, Pesina took a fighting stance. DiVita squeezed into a red robot helmet. Then, he lunged for his friend's neck. The two of them could barely contain their laughter.

Midway was filming a promo video for *Mortal Kombat 3*, which gave the *MK* digitization actors a chance to clown around for the camera. With increasing frequency, DiVita was not just throwing his mind into games but his body, too. DiVita was athletic, charismatic, and uninhibited—the perfect person to model for a game. At Midway, he had played the title character of a cancelled *Judge Dredd* game and cheered on cars in *Cruis'n USA* under the name Beefcake Boy. For *MK3*, he played the palette-swapped killer robots Sektor, Cyrax, and Smoke, as well as a Native American fighter named Nightwolf. To play the robots, he donned a costume patched together from BMX gear, ice hockey equipment, duct tape, and rubber tubing.

MK3 was Midway's marquee release in a marquee year: 1995, the year of *Mortal Kombat*. The company capitalized on the public's hunger for the franchise by signing deals left and right, leading to an animated movie, a touring stage show, and heaps of merchandise. August 18 marked a pinnacle in company history when New Line Cinema released a big-budget *Mortal Kombat* movie. This time, instead of Carlos Pesina, Christopher Lambert from the *Highlander* series slipped on Raiden's hat. For three weeks, the film was no. 1 at the box office. The whole Midway gang visited the theater to watch it together, then posed and goofed off for photos in the lobby.

Williams Bally/Midway was firing on all cylinders. New coin-ops like *Revolution X* and *Cruis'n USA* were crushing it. Midway also acquired the failing Atari

Games around that period, picking up the classic 80s series Gauntlet.

Williams Bally/Midway was a leader outside of arcade gaming, controlling 70 percent of the world market for pinball. It was also developing video lottery terminals for casinos, casual touchscreen games for bars, and networking technology for arcades so cabinets across the country could be linked for competitive play.

As the company was minting money, its financial reputation became white-hot. It attracted the interest of Sumner Redstone, the billionaire chairman of Viacom, Inc., who took a 25 percent stake in the company and hinted at taking on a bigger role. In late 1996, Williams Bally/Midway spun Midway off into its own company and put it on the stock market under the ticker symbol MWY.

A high score screen in the attract mode of the *MK3* upgrade *Ultimate Mortal Kombat 3* held two more important sets of initials. Reading spots 12 and 13 together spelled a message: *NBA TWO*.

There was never any doubt that Midway would keep making basketball games with or without its hit brand. Negotiating with the NBA all on its own, Midway secured a new license for a new game. The split between Acclaim and Midway was most evident at the Electronic Entertainment Expo in May 1996. In one booth on the convention floor, Acclaim promoted *NBA Jam Extreme*. In another, Mark Turmell and his team presented *NBA Hangtime*.

Morale on Turmell's team had taken a hit after losing the *NBA Jam* license—the reception to *WrestleMania* stung, too—but the grind of the arcade business meant that the next project was never far off. *Hangtime*'s flyer touted the two-on-two game as being from "the original *NBA Jam* design team," which included everyone but Goskie. Unlike the 3D take of *NBA Jam Extreme*, *NBA Hangtime* stayed close to *Jam*'s familiar look and feel. Midway brought Air Morris back for more slick moves and improved its digitization techniques. The team kept in the "on fire" mode, and threw in features like alley-oops, crossovers, outdoor courts, and team fire. The gameplay was cleaner and smoother. Jon Hey provided sound design again, and Chicago rapper M-Doc provided beats for the soundtrack. Instead of Tim Kitzrow, Chicago Bulls commentator Neil Funk called the action. Funk was fine: not as animated as Kitzrow but not as out of place as Marv Albert.

Hangtime's most innovative addition harkened back to the days Midway planned the first *NBA Jam*. Turmell had kicked around the idea of a Create-A-Player mode, but when they didn't have the time or space to put it in *Jam*, it found a home in *Hangtime*. For 50 cents, you could spend two minutes designing and refining your own player, adjusting their appearance and abilities to your whim. The gallery of heads had an assortment of monsters, weirdos, and real players.

Of course, the game had secret characters, too. The Midway staffers returned and were joined by additions like commentator Neil Funk, Chicago sports anchor Dan Roan, and *Friends* star Matthew Perry. When the team extended *GamePro* writer Dan Amrich an offer to be a character, Amrich was thrilled and asked to wear a funny pair of bunny ears for his shoot. The team didn't just sign off on the idea but loved it: Anything they could do to snag players' interest and give them something Acclaim couldn't was a positive.

NBA Hangtime arrived in May 1996. Between the original game and its upgrade *NBA Maximum Hangtime*, Midway sold about 15,000 cabinets. While strong numbers, the impact was nothing close to that of *NBA Jam. Hangtime* didn't make much of a splash on consoles either. While Acclaim invested millions in marketing, Midway management wanted to do as little marketing as possible. "We barely had a marketing group. We had a sales department. Sales people were not marketing people," Sal DiVita told me. Moreover, the marketing voices Midway did have did not know how to properly promote the game. *Hangtime* was the true sequel to a billion-dollar hit, but it had no ambitious campaign powering it. The home versions were doomed from the start by unappealing cover art of a generic player dunking with a deranged expression on his face. "The *Hangtime* box art was one of the worst box arts ever," DiVita said.

Development and marketing did, however, work in sync when it came to tapping into the idea of applying "exaggerated reality" to other sports. In the wake of *NBA*

Jam, another team at Midway released *NHL Open Ice: 2 on 2 Challenge* in 1995. *Open Ice* was an ice hockey game that beautifully combined the essence of *NBA Jam*—the speed, the colors, the fire, the feel—with NHL stars and a slippery rink. Midway promoted *NHL Open Ice* and *WWF WrestleMania* as Midway Sports Exclusives. More sports games were inevitable; by the late 90s, Midway would move an entire sports department into another building nearby. Turmell, for his part, wanted to try football.

Around 1994, shortly after *NBA Jam* took off, Midway began talks with the National Football League to acquire its license for a coin-op video game. Once again, Midway licensing director Roger Sharpe was responsible for negotiating the deal, but this took longer to broker than the one with the NBA. The NFL had unrealistic financial expectations, so Midway passed. After a spell, both parties returned to the table, and Sharpe signed the NFL to a deal that made sense for Midway.

The game, called *NFL Blitz*, would break ground for Turmell in a major way. For the first time, he was making a 3D game. This meant having to learn the programming language C instead of using the assembly language he had been writing games in for years. To generate the glossy polygonal graphics, the team worked with what they called "the Seattle System," a powerful game engine that used a high-end 3dfx chipset.

Digitization was out at Midway, and motion capture was in. Animator John Root arrived at Midway in time to join Turmell's team for *NBA Hangtime*, but his skills truly came into focus when it was time to work with the new tech. For *Blitz*, Root spent days at a computer motion-capturing the game's star player: Sal DiVita.

Wearing a skintight black suit dotted with tiny bulbs, he performed every possible action and gesture for the cameras around him, tossing his body every which way in a brightly lit room. In addition to everything you would expect from a normal football player, DiVita experimented with leg drops, splashes, and other pro wrestling moves. He had loved working on *WWF WrestleMania*, so he eagerly brought that intensity to football. More complex moves like a modified spinebuster, in which a player picked his opponent up by his mask then slammed him onto his back, allowed DiVita to get creative in new ways. DiVita wasn't just an actor in *NFL Blitz*—he was its lead artist, animator, and designer, too.

A far cry from the man who once refused to give Mark Turmell any fire graphics for *NBA Jam*, DiVita completely embraced the over-the-top sports aesthetic. His friendship with Turmell also flourished into a creative kinship. The two trusted each other's instincts and understanding of what worked in a Midway Sports title.

On the commentary side, Tim Kitzrow was back in the booth and pumped-up as ever. Increased memory meant more room for speech. In addition to short phrases like "Intercepted!" and "Touchdown!," he comfortably fit in longer ones like "Lights out, baby!"

and "Oh, he just levels him!" Calls were clearer and transitions were more polished than ever. *Blitz* allowed Kitzrow more room for creativity, too. Writing much of the script and improvising freely allowed Kitzrow to inject more of his own personality into the game and use the comedy chops he had spent years refining. This led to one-liners like "That was uncalled for... but a lot of fun to watch!"

Around late 1996, Jon Robinson from *GamePro* magazine met Turmell at an arcade convention. Turmel instructed Robinson, who ran *GamePro*'s "Hot at the Arcades" column, to visit a secret room that had a security guard at the door. "This is going to blow your mind," Turmell said. When Robinson entered the room, Turmell popped in a tape of his new game. NFL players sprinted across the screen in a lightning-fast game of football. The 3D action was impressive, but things got really interesting after the whistle. Players beat down one another with elbow drops, suplexes, neckbreakers, and other maneuvers. Someone picked up Green Bay Packers quarterback Brett Favre in a piledriver and slammed his head into the ground. If *Jam*'s signature move was the crazy slam dunk, *Blitz*'s was the brutal late hit. By the time the last bone crunched and the tape finished, Robinson's jaw was on the floor. He had only one thing to say: "Rewind."

In September 1997, *GamePro* debuted *NFL Blitz*, scoring an exclusive that came with screenshots, 3D art, and an interview with Midway. "Football is a big segment in the home market, but in the arcade, there have been very few football games and even fewer successful ones," Turmell said. "What we're doing is speeding things up by changing some of the rules."

Instead of the traditional eleven-on-eleven setup, *Blitz* was seven-on-seven. The game took you from playbook to field and back to playbook in a matter of seconds, and the fantastic graphics hurtled at 60 frames per second. Unlike the realistic bodies of *NBA Jam*, *NFL Blitz* players were more massive and muscular than their real-life counterparts. In the *GamePro* interview, Turmell teased that *Blitz* would be "the most violent football game ever designed." "There'll be some broken limbs," DiVita added, "but nobody's gonna get carried off the field."

Turmell had so much faith in his game that he called out the competition. "I think *Blitz* is going to be the number one arcade game," he declared, "and it's going to sell more units on the home side than Madden and GameDay combined."

NFL Blitz took two years to make—an eternity in coin-op—but it looked like a surefire hit. No amount of carnage was too much for the team—blood spattered off bodies, knees went into faces—and every enthusiastic reaction from a new player proved that *Blitz* would be a hit. Then, shortly before the game was scheduled to go on test, NFL representatives decided to see the game for themselves. The league had never signed off on the mayhem or really paid much attention to the project at all.

In Midway's office in Chicago, Turmell and DiVita met with the reps and demoed *NFL Blitz*. Assuming that their guests would not be happy with what they had done, they attempted to inflict as little damage as possible. Still, based on how it was designed, savagery was inevitable in *Blitz*. As the players smashed one another to a pulp after the whistle, the representatives looked on in horror. When the demo concluded, they excused themselves to talk. When they returned, they shared a dramatic decision: The NFL had to wash its hands of the entire project. "You can't have this violence," the reps told the developers. "If you want to ship this game, take our name off of it."

Losing the NFL license would be disastrous, but Turmell and DiVita took their vision of the game seriously. They negotiated with the NFL to remove the most vicious moves if they would see how the game performed on test. Turmell showed the reps a key piece of inspiration for *NFL Blitz*—a home video of the NFL's most brutal hits—which strengthened Midway's case for putting them in. Over the weekend, Midway and the NFL reviewed the moves together. When the reps saw DiVita's spinebuster in action, one of them exclaimed, "Are you guys fucking out of your minds?"

Owing to a miracle of compromise and oversight, *Blitz* eventually made it out—and it was a big hit. Selling roughly 13,000 units, *Blitz* reaffirmed Midway's status as the leader in arcade sports. Along with several successful home adaptations, the arcade game's popularity led to the coin-op updates *NFL Blitz '99* and *NFL Blitz 2000 Gold Edition*. *Blitz* '99 substituted two control panels for four, added an "on fire" mode, and allowed players to plug in their own Nintendo 64 memory cards to share *Blitz* data across formats, which was a piece of technology patented by Turmell and John Root. With *NFL Blitz*, Midway had a new franchise on its hands. The company was already taking steps to ensure that, unlike what happened with *NBA Jam*, *Blitz* would always stay with Midway, and asked the media to avoid using the "NFL" part of the game's name whenever possible.

Before long, Turmell and his team were back on basketball and bringing their brand of play to 3D. In another sign of how far Midway had come since having to convince the NBA that arcade games were worthwhile, *NBA Showtime: NBA on NBC* boasted two licenses at the same time. The phrase "NBA Showtime" had originated in a list of proposed names for *NBA Jam*, and the *NBA on NBC* affiliation meant Midway had access to branded graphics from the sport's broadcast leader, plus John Tesh's iconic "Roundball Rock" theme.

Unlike *NBA Jam Extreme*, *Showtime* transitioned *Jam* to three dimensions the proper way by juicing up the core two-on-two mechanic. For the first time, shoving your opponent too much sent him to the free-throw line, which triggered a mini-game about timed button presses. Willie Morris Jr. reprised his starring role again, but his moves were motion captured instead of digitized. Hand-drawn heads were a thing of the past. Now, face-mapping technology combined with headshots supplied by the NBA guaranteed accurate likenesses.

Tim Kitzrow returned in peak form, having refined his sportscaster persona. Kitzrow and Jon Hey worked on the pacing of the calls constantly until the commentary flowed naturally and the game felt like it could pass for a fast-paced TV broadcast. To psych himself up while making his calls, Kitzrow did his calls while looking at a photo of Scottie Pippen dunking on Karl Malone.

Arriving in arcades in March of 1999, *NBA Showtime* looked fantastic and sold well. The critical response was positive but not over the top, and the game quickly received home ports and an arcade update called *Gold Edition*. Soon after its release, Midway ironed out a deal with both the NFL and the NBA to put *NBA Showtime* alongside *NFL Blitz 2000 Gold Edition* for *Midway SportStation*, a single arcade cabinet allowed players to choose between the two games.

Combining two of the biggest sports leagues in the world into a single product was an incredible coup, and *Midway SportStation* was a testament to how far Turmell and DiVita's vision for Midway's sports brand had come.

But by the turn of the century, the game industry was rapidly changing. A tour de force like *SportStation* would have tilted the arcade world on its axis a few years earlier, but at that point, the team-up did little to move the needle for Midway. As a genre, arcade sports were getting overshadowed by a crowded field of simulation-style games that reveled in their faithfulness to how basketball actually played. Sims were generating all the excitement.

The popularity of coin-op games was falling dramatically, too. Developers and gamers sank their money and attention into the latest crop of consoles: the Sony PlayStation, Nintendo 64, and Sega Dreamcast. Each of those systems received a port of *NBA Showtime* that wasn't too far removed from the original, at least not enough to make it a necessity to experience the original. Midway's future as an arcade game company was murky, and the recent happenings on the pinball side were a dark omen.

In the early 1990s, Williams Bally/Midway had been on top of the pinball industry, rolling out one impressive table after another, including the enormously successful titles *The Addams Family* and *The Twilight Zone*. But as its video games raked in the change, Williams Bally/Midway's pinball earnings consistently lagged behind. By the end of the decade, the company was one of a tiny handful of pinball manufacturers left.

Neil Nicastro delivered an ultimatum to the pinball division: Innovate and create a game that sold like gangbusters or he would close the entire division. Since Williams made up so much of the market, it was a move that could effectively kill the pinball industry. As the entire enterprise hung in the balance, the brightest minds in pinball at Williams Bally/Midway collaborated on "Pinball 2000," a twist on the format that combined pinball with video graphics. The two Pinball 2000 games sold well but far from well enough. *Star Wars: Episode I - The Phantom Menace*, delayed from its movie tie-in release schedule, would be the last pinball table to leave the factory line.

In October 1999, Williams announced that it was officially done with pinball. Instead of selling the pinball division, the company halted all manufacturing and laid off around 200 workers. Slot and video gambling machines were proving to be an increasingly lucrative market, so the company turned its energies to those products. The plummeting sales of pinball games didn't indicate a creative failure as much as a cultural shift. Players were losing incentive to leave home.

Creatively, Midway's arcade division was still flourishing. Alongside its sports games, *Mortal Kombat 4*, and Cruis'n sequels, the company's late 90s releases included eye-catching and imaginative titles like *CarnEvil*, a horror-themed light gun shooter, and *Hydro Thunder*, an adrenaline-pumping speedboat racer. In 2000, Midway rolled out *The Grid*, an addictive third-person shooter designed by the Mortal Kombat team about a homicidal game show in the spirit of *Smash T.V.* Nothing took off. As coin-op revenues fell, Midway's stock was hit hard. The company funneled more resources into home adaptations and original console games. On March 6, 2001, the company announced that it had reduced its coin-op video game work force by about 60 employees, adding to the dozens let go in the year prior. The writing was on the wall.

On the cloudy Chicago morning of June 22, 2001, Midway sent out a second press release. Due to what it described as "ongoing declining demand in the coin-op arcade video game market," the company was leaving the arcade business for good. Midway cut yet another 60 or so jobs. Moving forward, home games would be the company's sole focus.

"On a purely consumer level, polygons killed arcades," *GamePro*'s Dan Amrich said to me. "When the PlayStation and N64 arrived, suddenly, you had home machines that were able to deliver the same kind of visual fidelity and innovation that coin-ops had traditionally provided." The success of inventive and immersive games like *Metal Gear Solid*, *GoldenEye 007*, and *The Legend of Zelda: Ocarina of Time* signaled the vast potential of home games. The internet growing into an increasingly accessible form of entertainment didn't help either.

A trip to the arcade had grown unsustainably expensive. Current games ran between 50 cents and a dollar per play, with the player seemingly paying more and receiving less time. Games were becoming increasingly fleeting and lightweight, relying on money-hungry mechanics and gimmicky controls over compelling gameplay. The selection of genres grew limited, with racers, shooters, fighters, sports games, rhythm games, and little else. As Amrich pointed out, consoles got rid of those pesky individual transactions you needed to make to play a coin-op game. With a home game, you could pay once and play forever.

Turmell was bummed to see the arcade division go, but DiVita was itching for a change. The coin-op business had brought the headaches of the politics of dealing with arcade distributors and salespeople, and how they bought games. "If they didn't get kickbacks," DiVita recalled, "they wouldn't promote your game." Now, Midway would get to give the people what it wanted and the people would get to buy what they wanted. "I was ready to shed the past as fast as possible," DiVita said. "I felt like there was too much corruption there, not realizing that the consumer market had far more corruption than the coin-op market."

Midway was optimistic about its future in the home market, but in time, the arcade business wouldn't be the only thing to disintegrate.

CHAPTER 11:
"THE NAIL IN THE COFFIN"

"You think I can make this?"

In a motion capture studio in Los Angeles, Shaquille O'Neal clasped a basketball. The basket was half a court behind him, but O'Neal couldn't resist a challenge.

A few feet away, Midway animator John Root sat by a computer, waiting for the system to come online. "No way," Root said. "You can't even make free throws, and you're going to make a half-court shot over your back on a 9½ foot rim?"

Shaq and Root were working together on *NBA Hoopz*, a spin-off of *NBA Showtime* exclusively for home consoles. Midway had paid Shaq a million dollars to capture his moves, be part of the game's cover shoot, and fulfill other promotional obligations. The slow speed of the motion-capture technology required a considerable amount of standing around, and the two of them had time to kill.

"Well, how much do you wanna bet?" Shaq asked.

"Five dollars," said Root.

Shaq scoffed. "Not worth my time."

Root thought he was being played, but the stakes raised quickly. The second Root said "fifty dollars," O'Neal launched the ball over his shoulder. The ball hit the rim, but it didn't go in. "You owe me fifty dollars," Root announced.

Ten minutes later, Shaq was on the other side of the backboard and offering another bet, which Root again took him up on. The day continued like this, with a dozen similar scenarios happening on different places around the studio. Shaq made some and missed some. "At the end of the day, he owes me $80, but I guess he doesn't carry cash," Root remembered. "If anybody knows Shaq, they need to tell him you still owe John Root $80 for that motion capture shoot."

Root's Shaq story was a bright spot at Midway during a time without many of them. All things considered, 2001 was the worst year in company history.

The year began with the understanding the arcade boom was long past and the industry was on a crash course. When Midway closed the division in June, it upended everything. Closing an entire wing would be a loss for any business, but coin-op games had been Midway's lifeblood. For the talent who had spent years at the company, making arcade games was a point of pride. Everything in the game industry used to follow in the footsteps of the arcade, but now it seemed as if the arcade wouldn't even have any footsteps to leave behind.

Midway's key console releases in 2001 were all ports, updates, and variations of arcade games. The lineup included *NBA Hoopz*, *Gauntlet: Dark Legacy*, and the Turmell-esque ice hockey game *NHL Hitz 20-02*. Mark Turmell had been spending his time on *NFL Blitz 20-02*, a new *Blitz* that was initially designed as an arcade game but had to have its high polygon count sacrificed when it went directly to the Sony PlayStation 2, Nintendo GameCube, and Xbox instead.

NFL Blitz 20-02 was scheduled to hit stores on September 17, 2001. Six days before its release, the United States was hit with the biggest terrorist attack in the country's history. "That jolted all of us. We slowed down," Turmell said. "It was a weird time. It was a tough time." The game missed its launch window and instead hit stores in February 2002.

Things had already been changing in other ways. Eugene Jarvis was gone, as were other Midway staples like *Terminator 2* programmer George Petro and *NBA Jam* audio director Jon Hey. In 1999, John Tobias and other *Mortal Kombat* staffers left Midway to launch their own company, Studio Gigante. In 2000, Midway laid off many employees, including licensing guru Roger Sharpe.

In June 2002, the *New York Times* ran a story by Jeremy Horwitz called "Mortal Apathy?" that spelled out how just bad business at Midway was. Seven of the fifteen games Midway released in 2001 sold 50,000 copies or fewer, a figure that included a Game Boy Advance version of *Mortal Kombat* that was absolutely savaged in reviews. As sales and its stock value plummeted, Midway closed the 2001 fiscal year at a loss of $78.4 million.

2002 wasn't looking so hot either. The company had forecasted one quarter's losses as being up to $10 million but had then had to revise that number to $12.5 million. *Mortal Kombat: Deadly Alliance*—Midway's first home-only entry in the main line of MK games—had been delayed from September to November, risking the loss of fall shopping season revenue. In a conference call, Neil Nicastro described one recent game's sales as "abysmal" and said that the company had "taken account of the fact that we've done a terrible job in predicting what's going to happen."

The next year, Midway lost another $116 million.

For Midway, being in coin-op wasn't just about bragging rights. There were practical benefits, too. Arcade games were made by small teams at low costs. Selling 5,000 units of a game at $3,000 apiece meant turning a profit, and selling anything past that was a bonanza. Creating console games required more people, more specialization, more tech, more releases, more time, more money, more everything. Midway transformed titles that started life as arcade games, such as the soccer game *RedCard 20-03*, into home games, but arcade games and home games were fundamentally different creative products. Instead of designing entertainment built to thrill for a few quarters at a time, developers had to make games that were robust enough to sustain dozens of hours of play and stand out in an immensely crowded marketplace. Midway wasn't a juggernaut any longer but just another company in the rat race, late to the game and out of its element.

Still, there were bright spots. *Mortal Kombat: Deadly Alliance* sold two million copies. Even though the series was losing ground to new fighting game franchises, MK was a reliable star property. Midway took successes like *Deadly Alliance* as cause to double down on the console market, bringing on new employees and even new game studios. Over the 2000s, the company operated or bought out studios in Chicago, Los Angeles, San Diego, Austin, Seattle, England, and Australia.

With new projects and a new look (having cut off his long trademark locks), Turmell was upbeat about the prospect of working with home technology for the first time since the 1980s. He and DiVita oversaw *MLB Slugfest 20-03*, an explosive baseball game in the *NBA Jam* mold. Tim Kitzrow came back for commentary, this time with Chicago radio DJ Kevin Matthews as a sidekick, and had a terrific time. Kitzrow got the chance to do entire comedic bits, further expanding his commentator character. *Slugfest*'s success jump-started a new sports series for Midway. Soon after, Turmell was ready to go back to basketball.

The NBA of the early 2000s looked like a very different place than the one of *NBA Jam*. The Chicago Bulls dynasty was over, Michael Jordan was in the twilight of his career, and stars like Shaq and Scottie Pippen had moved onto new teams. Players like Allen Iverson, Chauncey Billups, Vince Carter, Kevin Garnett, and Stephon Marbury represented the current wave. The era was one of lavish living: bling, big chains, big cars, braggadocious hip-hop, and homes worthy of *MTV Cribs*. This aesthetic drove Midway's latest game, *NBA Ballers*.

Instead of two-on-two, *NBA Ballers'* gameplay would be one-on-one, an idea that Turmell had been kicking around since first sketching out *NBA Jam*. *Ballers* made another alteration to the Midway basketball formula by awarding points for ball-handling, inventive combos, emphatic dunks, and moves that made your opponent look foolish. Instead of Willie Morris Jr., a handful of skillful players from the popular streetball brand AND1 came in for motion capture. You played on courts in a variety of settings: Kobe Bryant's villa, Scottie Pippen's yacht, Karl Malone's winter chalet. You could upgrade your basketball skills, as well as your house, clothing, and car. A variety of flamboyant vehicles were available, including Range Rovers and Cadillac Escalades.

Turmell relished the material and poured himself into the project. During the game's development, he reunited with his friend and old fan John Romero. The *Doom* and *Quake* co-creator had recently left id Software to join Midway's studio in San Diego and oversee a new *Gauntlet*. One time, Romero and Turmell went to lunch together, and Romero got to see Turmell's latest ride. "Because he was making *Ballers*," Romero remembered with a laugh, "he had to have an Escalade."

Released in 2004, *NBA Ballers* was a hot seller, launching a promising series. This was good news when Midway needed all the good news it could get. Its latest plans involved partnering with Criterion Software, a European company whose RenderWare graphics engine was going to be the technological ace in the hole Midway needed to compete in the home market. Then, Electronic Arts snapped up Criterion in 2004, and the RenderWare plans were dust. That same year, EA struck Midway another blow when it secured the exclusive rights to release video games with the NFL license. All of a sudden, *NFL Blitz* was finished.

Midway's strategy of building *Blitz* as a brand of its own would pay off. Over the years, the NFL had been putting more and more pressure on Midway to tone down the game's violent aspects, so with the loss of the license, Midway jumped at the chance to push the violence all the way back up—and further. 2005's *Blitz: The League* would be the first football game with a 17-and-up rating.

Developed by a new team led by Mike Bilder instead of Mark Turmell, the game centered on the seedy behind-the-scenes drama of a fictional pro league and its teams. Midway chief marketing officer Steve Allison called *Blitz: The League* "the ultimate alternative to watered down NFL-sanctioned football games." This game had dirty hits, excessive celebrations, off-the-field controversies, and stories about prostitutes. Vicious injuries, which were part and parcel of gameplay, could be treated with steroid injections—a story element that led to the game being banned in Australia. Midway also recruited notorious legendary linebacker Lawrence Taylor to lend his likeness and voice to Quentin Sands, the game's protagonist.

Like Shaq for *NBA Hoopz*, Taylor did not come cheap. Neither did any of the other huge names or licenses that were becoming integral to how Midway made and marketed their products. Iconic action director John Woo reunited with actor Chow Yun-Fat on *Stranglehold*, the video game sequel to their action thriller *Hard Boiled*. Dwayne "The Rock" Johnson lent his likeness to *SpyHunter: Nowhere to Run*, a reimagining of the Bally/Midway coin-op classic. *Nowhere to Run* was intended to be the basis of a *SpyHunter* film adaptation, but the game received a lukewarm reception and the movie was eventually scrapped. Midway also released video games based on The Lord of the Rings trilogy and the kids' movie *Happy Feet*.

At least one project was a calamitous failure. Midway teamed up with director John Singleton and Snoop Dogg for *Fear & Respect*, an ambitious and expensive *Grand Theft Auto*-style title. The game appeared on the cover of the January 2005 issue of *Game Informer* magazine. Bits of information on *Fear & Respect* trickled out until Midway abruptly axed the game in March 2006.

Major pushes for original Midway properties were few and far between, and exceptions like *The Suffering* and *Psi-Ops: The Mindgate Conspiracy* never graduated into franchises. Each of these games cost Midway millions of dollars to make, and neither found their footing. "It's one thing when you make a failure on the Genesis, but if you're putting out a triple-A title and it bombs, you can do only so many of those," *GamePro* writer Jon Robinson said. "It seemed like when other companies were tightening their belts, [Midway was] living it up."

As roles shifted and the faces changed, marketing plans began to drive the company's output instead of the designers. Power struggles between management and developers were constant. The developers were increasingly frustrated that people with no qualifications to make creative decisions were now determining what games would be made. Midway grew into an increasingly high-strung and dysfunctional work environment that was more hostile than productive. Competitiveness pushed camaraderie aside.

"When you take away the ability for people who have been successful to reach their visions the way they have done in the past, you're going to muddy up the results," Sal DiVita said. "We had moved around to where marketing was speaking for the market and telling design teams, 'This is what people are looking for.'" In the world of home games, promotion was more important, and Midway's marketing was still lacking. DiVita remembered the marketing team lecturing the developers on "over-the-top sports," the very house style the developers had come up with. "The marketing people would say, 'Midway is good at over-the-top games. Midway is good at doing sports games.' The reality is that Midway isn't good at doing anything," DiVita said. "It's the people. Mark is good at doing sports games. Boon and Tobias are good at doing fighting games. Midway is not a person. It doesn't have a brain. It doesn't know how to do anything."

For instance, Turmell felt he was hamstrung by management when designing the *NBA Ballers* sequel *NBA Ballers: Phenom* and that he couldn't make the creative decisions that he wanted. Turmell was pulled from the project, and he hung out in Chicago for months. In addition to his clashes with management, Turmell was going through a divorce, too. Midway encouraged Turmell to move to California and join its Los Angeles studio, where DiVita had also landed.

Midway's investors and creditors bailed the company out of money problems, but its debts kept piling up. In 2004, creditors sued the company. Neil Nicastro had stepped down as CEO in May 2003 during the company's fourth consecutive fiscal year of net losses, then left the company entirely in 2004. David F. Zucker came into Midway from ESPN and Playboy to replace him, but he had no experience in the video game industry and was received poorly.

Despite its efforts, Midway's games just weren't selling in the numbers required of a console game company. The current class of developers, while talented, didn't have the same chemistry or ingenuity as the Midway staff of the

90s. Teams had grown too big. Projects took too long and cost too much. The company felt rudderless.

John Romero's experience making *Gauntlet: Seven Sorrows* for Midway was a frustrating one due to his encounters with management. When the superstar game designer landed at Midway's San Diego office in the early 2000s to work on the latest Gauntlet game, Midway management indicated that it was committed to releasing games that got scores of 80 percent-plus or more on the review aggregator website Metacritic, meaning that gameplay was top priority. That was exactly what Romero wanted to hear, allowing him ample time for production and polishing on his work. In his year and a half at the company, he found that philosophy had been thrown out of a window, and Romero left Midway five months before it released *Seven Sorrows* in December 2005. "The people that ran the company," Romero said, "were crazy."

Venture capitalists and cash infusions couldn't stop the bleeding. Zucker was unable to turn the company around and resigned in March 2008. By October of that year, Matt Booty—a Midway veteran who started out working on sound and programming for games like *Mortal Kombat II* and *NBA Jam: Tournament Edition*— had unexpectedly risen to the rank of CEO.

NBA Jam team members Shawn Liptak and Jamie Rivett saw the signs of a company in collapse and left Midway in May 2007. Liptak believed that the company culture had grown too insular. Everyone was working on their own technology and tools without sharing them, meaning that it cost Midway far too much to develop games. "They lost money basically every quarter," Liptak remembered. "We had one quarter where we made a profit. Some quarters, we'd lose a little. Some, we'd lose a lot. I knew eventually it was going to end."

By late 2007, Viacom billionaire Sumner Redstone was Midway's majority shareholder. Taking a 25-percent stake since the mid-90s (an investment he made personally), the media magnate grew to own 87 percent of the company. As Midway went off the rails, Redstone took a greater role in the business.

In November 2008, the New York Stock Exchange threatened Midway with a delisting notice, giving them six months to recover before it pulled its poor-performing stock. The situation did not improve. Later that November, Redstone dumped all of his remaining stock and roughly $70 million in debt to Mark Thomas, a private investor, for just $100,000. This meant that Thomas shouldered tremendous debt but also stood to make a killing off a $30 million secured claim, meaning that he would be the first creditor to be repaid if Midway was to file for bankruptcy. Redstone had washed his hands of the sinking ship.

Looking from the outside in, Tim Kitzrow never saw any indication that the company was going downhill, but when the slide happened, it was fast. He spoke to Midway employees who were panicked by the company's stock bottoming out. It hurt Kitzrow, too, knowing that the company freely spent millions on *Slugfest* cover athletes like Alex Rodriguez and Sammy Sosa but often gave him a hard time on relatively paltry amounts. "While they're trying to save $5,000 with me, they're burning money on this and that," he recalled. "Lavish money was just thrown around, and I'm fighting for my life to get basic compensation."

By late 2008, Midway still pushed, even as things looked dire. *Mortal Kombat vs. DC Universe*, a comic book crossover fighting game by the MK team, was a big seller. So was *TNA Impact!*, a wrestling game Turmell and DiVita oversaw at Midway's office in Los Angeles. Despite the hard times, they felt that the quality of their games would justify the company's continued existence. "I never accepted that the glory days were gone," DiVita said. "We just kept on doing our thing. We were going to make something that will get a lot of attention. We just had to find our footing again."

On February 12, 2009, Midway announced that it was filing for Chapter 11 bankruptcy. In a statement, CEO Matt Booty called it a "difficult but necessary decision." The bankruptcy filing, he said, "will relieve the immediate pressure from our creditors and provide us time for an orderly exploration of our strategic alternatives." Turmell and DiVita watched the company burn down from California, helpless to stop it. Turmell never got to say goodbye to the building.

Seeing Midway's collapse was sad for everyone. Tim Kitzrow had been contracted to voice sequels to *NHL*

Hitz and *MLB Slugfest*. Suddenly, those contracts were gone, and he was back to waiting tables. His ride in the game business seemed as if it was over.

John Romero, meanwhile, knew Midway not just as the company he had worked for but as the name stamped on legendary games like *Pac-Man* and *Space Invaders* that he had grown up playing in the Bally/Midway era. Crashing and burning did not feel like a fitting finale. "That's what the idiots who run the company deserve but not the teams—because they were excellent teams," Romero said to me. "They had a legendary company and just tossed it in the trash."

Soon after filing Chapter 11, Midway's assets were auctioned off to repay its creditors. Warner Bros. Interactive Entertainment, who had worked with the company on games like *Happy Feet* and *Mortal Kombat vs. DC Universe*, purchased most of Midway's assets for $49 million. The sale included the rights to the Mortal Kombat franchise, which would keep Ed Boon's MK team intact as a new development group called NetherRealm Studios. Shortly thereafter, visiting midway.com took you to warnerbros.com.

In April 2009, Eugene Jarvis received a phone call. It was Matt Booty, Midway's last CEO, calling to let him know that a crew would be taking apart the offices the following day. If there was anything he wanted before the remnants of Midway were tossed out, now was the time to get it.

That evening, Jarvis and a group of Midway veterans assembled for a raid. They convened in the lobby of a corporate building in the back of the Midway complex next to the Chicago River. By that point, all the best stuff had been taken. Only scraps were left: game cartridges, marketing documents, telephones, stray pieces of furniture. The gang picked through the remains.

Something in the lobby caught Jarvis's eye. He noticed a framed poster outlining Midway's goals for success—one of the byproducts of the home game era. It had 29 bullet points on it. "No wonder they failed," Jarvis said to himself. "You can't do 29 things at the same time." He took the poster down and announced his plans to put it on eBay. Another raider was quick to stop him. "Whoever takes it will carry the failure of Midway with him," he said. "You have to throw this into the Chicago River." Jarvis reconsidered.

Later that night, the group headed to the riverbank with the poster in hand. This poster symbolized the worst of Midway: the hundreds of millions of dollars squandered, the thousands of jobs that had been lost, the terrible decisions that were made—all the opportunities to recover that had come and gone. The group recited a tongue-in-cheek prayer for Midway, then chucked the poster into the water.

In moments, the metal frame came apart. Then came the glass, then the foam board, and finally the paper itself. The letters in "Midway" and its 29 goals dissolved into the muddy water, traveling past 3401 North California Avenue down, down, down the Chicago River.

CHAPTER 12:
"LAUNCHES A SHOT"

In the 1990s, as one company invested millions in sports games that bent the rules, another spent its millions on sports games that did the opposite.

Going back to 1983 and bringing in Julius Erving to consult on *One on One: Dr. J vs. Larry Bird*, Electronic Arts strived to reproduce its subject with the utmost fidelity. This was not an easy task considering the technological limits of consoles at the time, but EA built a reputation as a powerhouse in sports simulations. *One on One*'s success led EA to create franchises like Madden for football and Triple Play for baseball. By the mid-90s, one of EA's marquee franchises was NBA Live, which allowed you to run real-life plays, manage a full roster, and sort through endless stats. Electronic Arts transformed an army of talented programmers and a stockpile of marquee licenses into EA Sports, an incredibly successful division that boasted, "If it's in the game, it's in the game."

Part of EA's brilliance was its mastery of planned obsolescence. Every passing year, EA would refresh its titles: *NBA Live 95* gave way to *NBA Live 96*, then *NBA Live 97*, and so on until EA Sports became the market leader in basketball games. Each release brought roster updates and improvements. The cycle created a steady stream of revenue—a model Acclaim attempted to copy with games like *NBA Jam '99* and *NBA Jam 2000*.

As consoles were able to do more and more, consumers began picking realistic and complex sports games over their arcade-style competitors. In 1998, Midway sold more than two million home copies of *NFL Blitz*, barely beating *Madden NFL 98*. Four years later, Madden had pulled far ahead, selling 3.75 million copies of its latest game to 200,000 of *NFL Blitz 20-02*. By the time Midway collapsed, EA Sports had a fiercer rivalry with 2K Sports, another publisher of simulations, than it did with Midway. In the war between the arcade-style sports game and the simulation, the sim had won.

To a lesser degree, Electronic Arts was developing an interest in arcade sports by creating less realistic games to supplement its key sim properties. In 2000, the company launched EA Sports Big, and the popularity of titles like *NBA Street*, *NFL Street*, and *SSX* proved that EA Sports was good at making an outrageous and playful game should the opportunity arise. The possibility of that opportunity was exactly why Trey Smith was there.

In 2009, Smith in his mid-thirties with almost a decade's worth of experience in the game industry. He had stumbled into the field: He grew up wanting to be actor, but when he got a gig playtesting the Tony Hawk's Pro Skater games, one thing led to another. After rising through the ranks at Activision, Smith took a position with EA Vancouver, the company's studio in Burnaby, British Columbia, Canada. His work included the skateboarding game *Skate*, the MVP Baseball series, and the goofy boxing game *FaceBreaker*.

That year, EA Sports executive producer Brent Nielsen recruited Smith to work on an all-new basketball game for the Nintendo Wii. The Wii and its revolutionary motion-gesture controls had lit up the industry, and *Wii Sports* was its breakthrough title. While *Wii Sports*'s versions of bowling and tennis were simple games, the control mechanic made the game a monumental hit. In this vein, EA was eager to do a casual hoops game where all it took to shoot, block, pass or steal was a flick of the wrist.

Smith and his team at EA Vancouver built a prototype starring two faceless mannequins called "Stickmen" who engaged in an infinite game of pickup. The simplicity of the prototype allowed the team to nail the fundamentals of gameplay and the responsiveness of the controls before doing anything else. All of the Stickmen's animations were based on classic *NBA Jam* moves, particularly the game's big dunks.

Over time, the team refined the prototype. When a shot clock and score-keeping feature went in, interest around the office soared. EA staffers hollered and shouted at each other while crowding the game. Smith knew they were onto something.

Early on, the project went by the working titles *NBA Bounce* and *NBA Kids* with the idea being that you would play as NBA players with gigantic heads. As the team expanded and fleshed out the game's details, Smith was struck with another idea. He sat down Nielsen and asked him: Why couldn't they just make this the new *NBA Jam*?

EA Sports checked in with the league to see who owned the license. As it so happened, the NBA did, and with Midway and Acclaim both out of business, the *NBA Jam* name was up for grabs. The two parties quickly brokered a deal, then EA made it official: *NBA Jam* was coming back, and Trey Smith was its creative director.

As someone who grew up playing *Jam* on the Super Nintendo with his brother, Smith couldn't believe his good fortune. Neither could the rest of the team, which was filled with *Jam* die-hards, like its lead designer Jeremy Tyner and art director Rob Hilson. The night they found out that *they were going to make NBA Jam*, everyone went out and partied. The next day, the cold truth stared them in the face: *They had to make NBA Jam*.

The solution was to employ "the sequel rule of thirds," a concept Smith described as a way to divide the game's design into three buckets. The project aimed to deliver a third that was the same (In Smith's words, "Take them back to their happy place"), a third that was improvements ("Don't muck with the recipe, enhance it"), and a third that was all new ("Take the game places it has never been before").

From the outset, Smith's team of twenty or so swore by the motto, "Be true to *Jam*." This meant taking cues from the arcade version of *NBA Jam: Tournament Edition* and nothing past it. The look, sound, and feel of the new *NBA Jam* had to echo the original, not only because the game targeted nostalgic fans but also because *Jam* did so many things right. The breakneck two-on-two experience would be great for a four-player Wii game.

Days into development, Smith heard the most amazing coincidence. EA Tiburon, the company's Florida branch, had just hired Mark Turmell. After a brief stint at THQ, Turmell had been hired by EA to find ways to make the *Madden* and *NCAA Football* games simpler and more accessible. The *NBA Jam* team introduced themselves to Turmell and asked to pick his brain. Turmell was happy to chat, so they scheduled a video conference.

Smith, Nielsen, Tyner, and Hilson signed onto Skype. When Mark Turmell appeared in the little window, Smith thought, "Holy cow, he is a big guy." The EA team intended to show him Turmell an *NBA Jam* presentation they had pitched to executives, but the call was plagued with technical difficulties. Instead of being able to do the presentation they wanted, they sent over a couple of videos and improvised explanations. Turmell listened and sat patiently through the technical issues. Once the EA team finished, it was eager for his feedback. "I think you guys are barking up the right tree," he said. Then, Turmell offered to come to Canada.

A week later, Turmell's plane touched down in Vancouver. Although he was only at the office briefly, Smith was thrilled to discuss the nitty-gritty of game development with him. Smith found Turmell's knowledge and memory to be outstanding; he *still* remembered *NBA Jam*'s probability tables and what the difference between a 7 and 8 on a dunk stat meant. He was perfect for EA's vision of *NBA Jam*. "We wanted the OG," Smith recalled to me. "We wanted the magic."

Visually, the new *NBA Jam* mimicked its predecessors, with a fixed TV-broadcast-style perspective of the court and characters who had distinctive faces. While watching *South Park*, Smith had the idea to give *NBA Jam* three-dimensional player bodies with flat two-dimensional heads. Leveraging EA Sports' contract with Getty Images, a stock photo service that had an almost infinite library of NBA player photos, would be pivotal. If LeBron James ran down the court in the new *NBA Jam*, you would see his actual face from a Getty shot. Similarly, if he winced when he was shoved in the game, that expression came from the real James, too. This allowed for a variety of expressions for a variety of situations. Management was skeptical of the idea, but once the concept was put into practice with blurs to transition the expressions, the look popped.

The next key piece to figure out was the commentary. The team *had* to get the original voice of *NBA Jam*, but where would they even find Tim Kitzrow? Somebody hopped on Facebook and found him in seconds. Minutes later, they were messaging back and forth with Kitzrow, then talking to him on the phone. Kitzrow, elated to hear about the remake, let out a hearty "BOOMSHAKALAKA!"

At the time, Kitzrow was working both lunch and dinner shifts at two restaurants in Chicago. He figured his ride in the game business had ended with Midway and he was another name on the scrap heap. The offer from EA Sports was manna from heaven. The company flew him to Vancouver, picked him up in a limo, and brought him to its multimillion-dollar facility. When Kitzrow arrived, a huge crowd of employees awaited his arrival for autographs and photos. "Would you mind taking a moment?" they asked. "Are you kidding me?" Kitzrow thought. "I just came from working double shifts five days a week, and here's 30 people in this palace lined up with *NBA Jam* memorabilia."

Over eight days, Kitzrow recorded approximately 50 times the audio of the original *NBA Jam*. He worked in a high-end recording booth, a far cry from the old meat locker at Midway. He wore a scarf and drank tea to preserve his voice, and kept the energy level high at all times. "There was no phoning it in for Tim Kitzrow," Smith said. "There was *one* take during all our recordings where his voice cracked."

Kitzrow had not only a huge amount of space to work with but the creative control to fill it how he liked. In addition to reprising the classics, Kitzrow said new phrases like, "The bigger the shove, the bigger the love," "Stuffed like a Thanksgiving turkey!," "First the shaka, and now the boom!," "He got his degree from Dunk'n-On-U!," and—if a player was hesitating as the clock was running out—"Sweet potato casserole, shoot it!" Transitions between phrases flowed naturally, and sometimes Kitzrow would go into bits, his comedic timing shining brightly.

The team made sure to throw in other classic *NBA Jam* staples, like an "on fire" mode, a Big Head Mode, and secret characters. Several classic *NBA Jam* players returned as special guests, as did team mascots, the Beastie Boys, and a fella by the name of Mark Turmell. In a nod to their iconic appearances in the home games, Bill and Hillary Clinton came back, and were joined by a bevy of other politicians, including presidents George W. Bush and Barack Obama.

EA improved on the classic Jam formula by adding crossovers and spin moves as a way to counter shoves, which gave the gameplay a new wrinkle. New modes allowed the company to get really creative. In "Backboard Smash," each team was represented by a glass backboard with its own health bar. Players traded shots and slams, working to whittle down their opponents' backboard meter until a good dunk shattered it to pieces. Boss battles granted you the opportunity to go one-on-one with a cast of NBA legends, each with his own special powers and pattern that needed to be exploited. Shaq, for example, literally fell from the sky and hit the Earth with an epic dunk; your task was to shatter the backboard before he could. Magic Johnson appeared to be made of actual magic—vanishing, teleporting, and passing to himself in front of your eyes.

Refining the gesture controls took a lot of work. The team hoped this novelty would incentivize new audiences to try *NBA Jam*, but in case anyone wanted more traditional controls, it also programmed in button configurations for the Wii controller joypad.

Once the fundamentals were sorted, the team moved on to roughly 50 items that they called the "Turmell Hit List." These were subtle elements that the team didn't figure out by dissecting *Tournament Edition* but instead had come from Turmell himself. Though off the planned schedule, these were items they needed to input to maintain their mantra of "Be true to *Jam*." Turmell broke down a variety of disparate points, such as why it was crucial to speed players up when they went off screen (so they could return to the action quicker), and why goaltending should not work properly 100 percent of the time (so the players had something to squabble over). The game, he insisted, *needed* to be 60 frames per second versus the assumed 30 frames per second, which would be very difficult to pull off. The frame rate, which Turmell could tell by sight, was crucial to emulating the smooth visuals of the original game. "It needs to be 60," Turmell told Smith. "I truly believe this game will fail if it isn't 60 frames per second."

Because Turmell wasn't going to budge, EA's *NBA Jam* ended up shipping at 60 frames per second and looked all the better for it. "It was just one of the challenges that the team overcame. The team was able to rally and deliver it and be that much more proud," Smith said. "I can honestly say we did everything we could to do *NBA Jam* justice. I have a smile on my face because we did not screw it up."

On October 5, 2010, *NBA Jam* arrived on the Nintendo Wii. It scored big. *Nintendo Power* put the game on its cover and described it as "one of the greatest comebacks in video game history" while the website Joystiq called it "a well-composed love letter to those who belonged to the culture of its predecessor." *USA Today* interviewed Smith and Turmell, and teased the story on the front page of the paper. There was revitalized interest in the game's secret characters. When EA Sports head Peter Moore appeared on Fox News to discuss politicians like President Obama and Sarah Palin appearing in *NBA Jam*, Fox News host Jenna Lee asked, "Is this a bipartisan game, though, Peter, because I read that the president has some special skills; do any of the Republicans have any special skills?"

During the game's production and promotion, the excitement surrounding *NBA Jam* indicated that EA Sports might need to do something more with the franchise than the single Wii game. Smith took one exchange at the 2010 PAX Prime convention as a sign. At EA Sports's booth, Smith introduced a shy couple dressed as Link and Zelda from *The Legend of Zelda* to two enthusiastic guys wearing backward baseball caps and jerseys that read "Bro Gamers," and encouraged the pairs to compete in a demo of *NBA Jam*. Link and Zelda were reluctant at first but did agree, and the game started on a polite if reserved note. Smith turned away for a few minutes to talk to someone else, and when he looked back, Link, Zelda and the Bro Gamers were high-fiving one another and chatting away. Once their interaction ended, they hugged each other before going their separate ways. Based on these kinds of reactions, Smith and his team knew their *NBA Jam* had the potential to be an even bigger project than they thought. They had to break this thing out.

NBA Jam hit the PlayStation 3 and Xbox 360 on November 17, 2010. While the PS3 and Xbox 360 releases were essentially the same game as the Wii edition, their launches were hurt by EA Sports making major changes to their release plans. At first, three single- and multiplayer modes of *NBA Jam* were to be packaged with *NBA Elite 11*, the company's latest basketball simulation. *Elite* would receive a standard physical release at $59.99 and *Jam* would be downloadable for free via a packaged-in scratch-off code. But after *NBA Elite 11* developed a terrible reputation online due to a buggy demo, the plan went downhill. *Elite* was delayed due to what EA President Peter Moore described as "concerns about gameplay polish," then was cancelled entirely—with the exception of a little-loved iOS version. Ultimately, EA Sports never released a console basketball sim in 2010 while its competitor Take-Two Interactive sold around four million copies of *NBA 2K11* without any competition. The situation was a fiasco, and *NBA Jam* suffered the blowback. The PS3 and Xbox 360 versions of *Jam* ended up receiving physical releases and a price point of $49.99, taking *Jam* from being a bonus game to being sold for almost as much money as the *Elite/Jam* bundle would have sold for.

Despite the major changes, the versions sold well on wide release and received positive reviews. In the spirit of *Tournament Edition*, the PS3 and Xbox 360 received an update of the game titled *NBA Jam: On Fire Edition*. Released in October 2011, it featured revitalized rosters and a thousand new gameplay improvements and additions, such as allowing both players to get on fire simultaneously and a "tag mode" where one player would automatically control whichever teammate had the ball. It, too, was a success.

Mobile versions of *NBA Jam* followed in 2011, 2012, and 2013, but after the release of *On Fire Edition*, updates from EA Sports about *NBA Jam* grew more seldom. In April 2012, the official @nbajam

Twitter account went dark; a month later, so did its Facebook page. In February 2014, @nbajam suddenly awoke and posted, "Retweet if you're ready for a new *NBA Jam*!" The next day, the tweet was gone, with an EA representative describing it as "unauthorized use of the *NBA Jam* Twitter handle" and clarifying that it had no announcements to make at the time. Since the company's roster update for the mobile games in 2015, the NBA Jam franchise remains in limbo. Its social media pages are strewn with instances over the years of fans asking EA Sports for a new Jam or if they could at least update the rosters, but the company remains silent.

Smith can't put his finger on why EA Sports abandoned *NBA Jam*, but his guess is that it has probably tried to do something but nothing materialized. His team's *NBA Jam*, Smith said, was a financial success, as it was cheap to make and far surpassed expectations. "It smoked every console version, barring the SNES and Genesis," Smith said, referencing other games in the cumulative NBA Jam series. The Android port racked up between 500,000 and a million downloads, and *NBA Jam: On Fire Edition* crept in and out of the top 20 downloads on the PlayStation Store for years after its release.

If Electronic Arts does return to NBA Jam, it likely won't be with Trey Smith or Mark Turmell. In 2011, Turmell left EA Sports Tiburon. Three years later, Smith left EA Sports Vancouver. One of Smith's motivations for moving on was, in fact, Turmell, whose ability to recognize opportunities and move around within the industry inspired Smith to do the same.

Smith is fond of many memories of working on the 2010 *NBA Jam*: his candid conversations with Turmell; the time the game got the cover of *Nintendo Power*; the moments he watched it soar at conventions; and, at one show, being visited by none other than Ed Boon, who wanted to meet the guy who brought NBA Jam back and did it right. Smith's team still keeps in touch and goes out for drinks, even though only one of them remains at EA. The group's cohesion and camaraderie changed how Smith manages projects and looks at game-making itself. "It was a special team," Smith said, "and it was a true joy to go to work every day."

Sources point to EA Sports holding the NBA Jam license through at least 2019. Any conversation of EA making a new game or a new licensee coming in is, at this moment, conjecture or preemptive. Still, Smith is confident that *NBA Jam* will return again. "It sat dormant for a really long time before we picked it back up. Maybe it's just going to take another team jumping in way over their heads," he said. "I'm anxious to see the next time it pops up. I hope they do it right."

CHAPTER 13:
"SWISH"

ONE NIGHT IN MARCH 2015, James Harden sprinted down the hardwood in Houston, ball in hand, as he often did. The Rockets superstar was feeling especially in the groove that Thursday. When Harden carved through the Denver Nuggets' defense and landed at the hoop, the impact was seismic. A familiar voice rang through the arena: "BOOMSHAKALAKA!"

Tucked into a control booth inside the Toyota Center, Tim Kitzrow watched the action closely, a headset microphone resting on his head. The moment was intense. His voice had just projected to a crowd of 18,000 NBA fans. On the Rockets' invitation, Kitzrow spent the evening delivering his classic lines to plays as they happened. His *NBA Jam* announcer persona had reached its highest form. Life was imitating a game that imitated life.

Kitzrow received all sorts of opportunities to think on his feet. When a Nugget launched an airball, he shouted, "Can't buy a bucket!" When another's shot was blocked: "Re-jected!" When a woman pushed the guy next to her away during the "kiss cam" fan segment: "Get that stuff out of here!" Kitzrow had to pinch himself. Were the words he was saying really coming out of the loudspeakers?

Houston was celebrating a special throwback night and holding a ceremony to commemorate the team's 1993 and 1994 championship lineups. Many of the era's players, including *NBA Jam* alumni Hakeem Olajuwon and Clyde Drexler, were in the house, as was league commissioner Adam Silver.

James Harden was on fire the whole game, and the atmosphere was hot. During a pause in the third quarter, a pre-recorded video of Kitzrow calling more Rockets action played on the giant screen overhead. "Are you tired of your old MVP?" Kitzrow pitched as Harden showed off. "This is a limited time TV offer. It slices, it dices, it dunks in your face—the amazing Hardenizer! (Beard sold separately.)"

Houston defeated Denver that night, but it was an even bigger win for Harden, who notched a career high 50 points in a game. The Houston staff who brought Kitzrow in said that he and *NBA Jam* had brought good luck. "That was the highlight of my career," Kitzrow said, remembering that night. Since then, other teams such as the Washington Wizards, the L.A. Clippers, and the Charlotte Hornets have hired Tim Kitzrow's services. For the Golden State Warriors, Kitzrow has voiced a recurring video segment called "Dub Jam."

Unlike the looks of an actor whose appearance changes with age, Kitzrow's voice has stayed as young as ever, and he maintains a career doing radio commercials and voiceover work. He has the rare distinction of having done commentary for video games for each of the "big" four American sports leagues: the NBA, the NFL, MLB, and the NHL. In 2017, he did commentary for *Mutant Football League*, a multi-platform sequel to the Sega Genesis classic *Mutant League Football*. He's always looking for new opportunities to work with pro teams, and he's bursting with ideas for new things based on *NBA Jam*: an energy drink called "Boomshakalaka," *Jam*-inspired sneakers, or apparel for Kitzrow's institution of higher learning, "Dunk'n-On-U". On the website whosaidwhatnow.com, he will record your voicemail greeting for $25; for $50, you can get a custom message or a birthday shout-out.

Kitzrow has always enjoyed performing his iconic role, but it took him time to take pride in it. When he got together with other actors at reunions and they talked about their television gigs, he didn't know what to make of a video game being his calling card. He never considered the impact and value of his persona until years later. "Once I found this home in video games, I was like, 'Oh, I can write, perform, create the character. Maybe this is what it was supposed to be.' I knew that I shouldn't be waiting tables my whole life," he said. "I have achieved some success and happiness by following that little inner voice."

NBA Jam is frequently regarded as one of the best arcade games, sports games, and even video games of all time. In April 2018, *Game Informer* magazine counted down the top 300 games of all time, putting the original *Jam* at no. 41. Players still participate in *NBA Jam* tournaments and rewrite the code of the home games to add new players. Along with updated team rosters, these editions have brought the likes of Kanye West, David Hasselhoff, "Hollywood" Hulk Hogan, the T-800 from *The Terminator*, and Super Mario to the court. Some have rewritten history and, at last, put Michael Jordan in *NBA Jam*.

NBA Jam is ingrained in pop culture. It has inspired T-shirts and Halloween costumes, research papers and comedy sketches, fine art and tattoos, beer and fireworks. People are always trying to find new ways to translate to *NBA Jam* to present day and even real life. Sportswriters occasionally imagine what current-day *NBA Jam* lineups would look like. Fans alter contemporary NBA highlights to look like gameplay from *Jam*. There have been at least three basketballs literally set on fire in tribute to the game.

All of the original game's storefront arcade habitats are long gone—Dennis' Place for Games on West Belmont is now a nightclub, the Kentucky Arcade in Lexington now a coffee shop—but a new form has taken their place: the arcade bar. With the decline of the traditional arcade business, the aging of *NBA Jam*'s audience, and the rise of the arcade bar format, these places have been instrumental in keeping the original coin-op game visible. *NBA Jam* cabinets draw nostalgic joy and competitiveness out of players, especially when alcohol gets involved.

In the NBA, the game still has admirers like Chris Paul, Dwight Howard, Kyle Korver, and Iman Shumpert. When the American basketball team visited Spain in 2014 for the FIBA Basketball World Cup, Golden State Warriors guard Stephen Curry brought along an Xbox 360 and *NBA Jam*. Houston Rockets forward/center Kenneth Faried played against Curry and was reminded of the countless hours he spent with his cousins on *NBA Jam* as a kid. When Faried closed his eyelids to sleep at night, he would still see the game vividly. *Jam* takes him back to, in his words, "a simpler time." "I would just come home and play video games all day," Faried said to me. "Schoolwork and making sure I cleaned my room was the most I had to worry about in life."

NBA Jam still has fans of all stripes all elsewhere. There's *Tonight Show* host Jimmy Fallon, actor Seth Rogen, Broadway supernova Lin-Manuel Miranda, and Seattle Seahawks quarterback Russell Wilson. In hip-hop, *NBA Jam* has been referenced by rappers like Redman, Del the Funky Homosapien, Too $hort, and Chip Tha Ripper. For his song "No More Parties in L.A.," Kanye West sampled a cheering sound effect from *NBA Jam*.

The world of sports video games is one of constant churn, but the star-studded rosters of *NBA Jam* and *NBA Jam: Tournament Edition* remain distinct, those headshots on the Team Select screen filling a digital yearbook of the era. Midway's arcade games and Acclaim's home ports represent *NBA Jam* in the cultural consciousness, the brand confusion and bad sequels having washed away with time. Shaquille O'Neal still has his first cabinet sitting in his home in mint condition. "It's an awesome game," Shaq said. "I think they need to bring it back."

The seven Midway staffers who made *NBA Jam* went their separate ways long ago, but each remains in the game business to varying degrees. Jon Hey, for example, teaches at DePaul University and writes music for Stern Pinball, Chicago's last pinball manufacturer, while Tony Goskie remains on Mortal Kombat at NetherRealm Studios. Everyone remembers *Jam*'s development and mind-boggling success fondly. "Personally, *NBA Jam* was the pinnacle of my career. I don't expect to replicate that for the rest of my life," programmer Shawn Liptak said. "It's one of those magic moments where the right place, the right time, and the right stuff came together to make that product."

Today, the building at 3401 North California Avenue still stands, albeit with its insides gutted and redesigned for a new business (reportedly, a veterinary clinic). In 2013, Scientific Games Corporation bought WMS Gaming, the slot machine business that was the last key piece of Williams Bally/Midway, and then moved out around 2018. There's only one indication of the coin-op empire that once stood there. A sign at the intersection of North California and West Roscoe reads "Honorary

Louis J. Nicastro Way" in tribute to the company's longtime chairman of the board and the man who once paid $7 million to keep Midway's goddamn name alive.

But drive fifteen minutes outside the city to a quiet industrial area with cracked pavement, and the sun never set on the dream of the arcade. In fall 2001, two months after Midway closed its arcade division, Eugene Jarvis opened Raw Thrills, Inc. in the neighboring village of Skokie. Williams Bally/Midway's original mastermind now runs one of the last coin-op video game companies in the country—and certainly its biggest. Head for any movie theater arcade or family entertainment center and you're bound to see a Raw Thrills logo somewhere.

Raw Thrills has made games based on an array of licenses, including Batman, The Walking Dead, Halo, and Jurassic Park. Some games even echo Midway, like a shooter based on *Terminator Salvation* and the colorful racing game sequel *Cruis'n Blast*. Most of its licenses have been secured by Roger Sharpe, who runs his own creative services agency and still relishes the thrill of the hunt decades after making the *NBA Jam* license happen. "It's something I am familiar and comfortable with. I value a lot of those relationships," Sharpe said. "It's a challenge, and every project is unique unto itself."

Raw Thrills does all of the software, programming, art, and mechanical engineering for its games on site. Jarvis also partners with Play Mechanix, a successful coin-op company founded by *Terminator 2* programmer George Petro after he left Midway in 1995, which itself is responsible for the hit *Big Buck Hunter* series. Both Petro and Jarvis are still in love with the format. Whether the business grows or shrinks, Jarvis's loyalty remains unshakeable. "At some point in your life, you just decide who the hell you are and what you do," Jarvis said, chuckling. "You stick with it until you go broke or die—one or the other."

The business isn't easy—competition from home games is fierce, while budgets and potential earnings are smaller—but for the first time in a while, Jarvis sees his industry on the upswing. "In the last two or three years, there's actually been real growth in the arcade market," he said. "It's crazy. I never thought I would live to see the day that arcades are expanding again, but they are."

In addition to the electronic medium, the word "arcade" is now associated with a style of simple pick-up-and-play games—the most popular of which are on mobile devices. A few Midway staffers share the sentiment that if the company had weathered 2009, it could have gone on to prosper in the mobile market. At its height, Midway thrived at every element crucial to mobile games: the vibrant visuals, the addictive mechanics, the ability to feed your impulses for a few minutes and dollars at a time. Fittingly, mobile devices are where Sal DiVita and Mark Turmell find themselves today.

After a stint at THQ, which included serving as creative director on an over-the-top wrestling game called *WWE All Stars*, DiVita has bounced around from company to company. He worked on the *Killer Instinct* sequel for the Xbox One, then took a management role at Spiral Toys to work on Wiggy, a piggy bank app with gamification elements to make learning about money fun for kids. He picks up things here and there, and is more interested in short-term projects. "My interest is in creating something entertaining, something that is a compelling mechanic," he said. "I like the idea of taking an older genre and coming up with a twist—some way of elevating it." Along those lines, he misses making arcade sports games, but he would only want to come back if he could add something new.

His friendship with Mark Turmell is still going strong. They live just a few miles apart from one another in the suburbs of San Diego and find time to get together even with their busy lives. On a recent Labor Day, DiVita visited Turmell, his wife Maria, and their children for a party; in addition to eating delicious food, Mark and Sal played *Fortnite* with the kids. "Even today, we have our heated debates and still know that five minutes later, we're just going to be talking about something else and everything is good," DiVita said. "We have a bond where we get the other person and respect each other."

In 2011, after leaving EA Sports, Turmell joined Zynga, the mobile game juggernaut behind ultra-popular titles like *FarmVille* and *Words with Friends*. As Senior Creative Director, Turmell leads teams who make match-three games. He's overseen massive successes like *Bubble Safari*, which once boasted an astronomical 14.8 million monthly active users. Turmell continues to work with licenses, developing games based on *The Wizard of Oz*, Willy Wonka, and Harry Potter. The job is satisfying, and has even reunited him with Midway alumni John Tobias and Jamie Rivett.

Turmell keeps in touch with his friend and mentor Eugene Jarvis, too; when Jarvis received an industry achievement award in 2014, Turmell was the one who presented him with the award. On a recent trip to Chicago, Turmell toured Raw Thrills's operation and was amazed at how they are keeping the business alive. The Midway nostalgia was powerful. "I miss coin-op a lot," Turmell said. "But everything I do is still trying to hook people in the first 60 seconds. The same attention span was there in the arcade: You had one quarter to get them."

Now more than ever, the data overflows. Without having to sort through audit sheets or sit with a notebook in an arcade, he can easily access a wealth of analytics breaking down how players react to every element of gameplay. Seeing and interpreting the data can be a learning experience, and Turmell is invigorated by the mobile medium and intent on looking forward. He is still tweaking—endlessly, constantly tweaking—his code in pursuit of the most compelling and entertaining experience, still sneaking in tricks and jokes when possible. He still wants the player to feel empowered. To that end, he still has the first game that made him feel empowered. At home, Turmell still keeps his Christmas gift from 1973: the *Pong* console his parents got him from Sears, complete in box with a price sticker of $99.99.

For all his ambition and continued success, Turmell knows that *NBA Jam* was his highest peak. "There were a few years where I thought, 'This is sad. I'll never top this.' How do you top that?" he said. "But now, I appreciate how it's been kept alive." On occasion, he will order something and someone will recognize the name Mark Turmell and thank him for something they loved as playing as a kid. Oftentimes, someone will drop him a message of appreciation out of the blue.

If you want to find Turmell nowadays, you don't need to go to the library for a phonebook or call long distance. All it takes is a good Google search. He's on Facebook, where Randolph Vance still wishes him happy birthday every March 22 whether Facebook reminds him or not.

On LinkedIn, Turmell keeps another profile—this one featuring a close-up of him with short hair, those flowing locks long gone. The page only skims his history in the game business, but it shows a developer whose passion for play still burns as brightly as it did in a basement in Bay City. "I love the process of making games, and of solving problems. Making people laugh or wince from the onscreen action is my drug," Turmell writes in his bio. "I am addicted to it."

NOTES

NBA Jam (THE BOOK) is the product of 68 exclusive interviews; access to original documents, photographs, and videos; and hundreds of hours spent researching *NBA Jam* in magazines, books, websites, forums, podcasts, videos, and wherever else I could find. The sources listed below played an important role in providing quotes, fleshing out stories, and corroborating details throughout this story. My thanks goes out to all these writers/creators and their outlets for their hard work and valuable contributions to documenting gaming history.

Harold Goldberg's *All Your Base Are Belong to Us: How Fifty Years of Videogames Conquered Pop Culture* (Three Rivers Press, 2011) and Steven L. Kent's *The Ultimate History of Video Games* by (Three Rivers Press, 2001) proved enormously helpful for narrating the early history and contexts of video games. The Arcade Flyer Archive (flyers.arcade-museum.com), MobyGames (mobygames.com) and Giant Bomb (giantbomb.com) reliably provided images, dates, and details for titles explored in this book.

Prologue: Attract Mode

The physical dimensions of the *NBA Jam* arcade cabinet are recorded in the official *NBA Jam Operations Manual* from January 1993, hosted at the Games Database: https://bit.ly/34fFP7B.

Details and descriptions of Dennis' Place for Games come from anecdotal sources, video, and "Arcade plays some fun games with writer's head" by Andy Rathbun for the *Chicago Tribune*, published October 17, 2003: https://bit.ly/2Y1lKxT. Additional info comes from "Gone but not forgotten: stores, and one arcade" written by *Time Out* editors along with Joel Reese, and compiled by Laura Baginski for *Time Out Chicago*, published September 9, 2014: https://bit.ly/2J7tBpy.

Chapter 1: "Here's The Tip"

Pong sales figure of 19,000 units comes from David Winter's website PONG-Story: http://www.pong-story.com/arcade.htm.

Information on *TV Basketball* and the early days of Midway comes from Keith Smith's "Video Game Firsts??", posted November 22, 2013 to The Golden Age Arcade Historian: https://bit.ly/2GYu7Vu.

Information on the background of *One on One* comes from "Profiles in Programming: Eric Hammond" by Matt Yuen for *St. Game,* vol. 4, March/April 1984 issue, hosted at the Internet Archive (https://bit.ly/2VIORbP) and at the Computer Gaming World Museum (https://bit.ly/2Zbz8DY).

Additional information comes from "How Dr. J and Larry Bird Helped Build a Video Game Empire" by Patrick Sauer for VICE Sports, May 25, 2017: https://bit.ly/2Ve76ql.

St. Game's review of *One on One* describing it as "a game that feels like the real thing" comes from the "Fairgame" section in vol. 4. March/April 1984.

Chapter 2: "From Downtown"

Details on Eugene Jarvis come from "This Game Industry Pioneer Never Gave Up on the Video Arcade" by Chris Kohler for Wired, December 18, 2013. https://bit.ly/2XZCTIi.

Game industry revenue figures during the Atari Crash are widely reported, such as in Randy McDaniel's "Sioux Falls Suffered Through Crash of 1983 Along With Rest of Country," published January 10, 2017 on KXRB.com: https://bit.ly/2KFsHAV.

The sales figures for *Defender* (60,000), *Robotron: 2084* (19,000), and *Blaster* (500) are provided by The Dot Eaters article "Defender and Vid Kidz - Brightly Coloured and Extremely Loud": https://bit.ly/2Zyqq3L.

Information on the Williams team in the 1980s comes from "Play Mechanix: The saviours of the arcade scene" by Damien McFerran for RedBull.com, May 28, 2014: https://win.gs/2H2jJMs.

Information on the development of *Arch Rivals* and Brian Colin/Jeff Nauman's partnership comes from "Along the Way" on Game Refuge's company website: https://bit.ly/2Y5wjQJ.

Chapter 3: "Magic Carpet Ride"

Details on Mark Turmell's early life and career come from a wide variety of published sources: "Pre-Game Interview: Mark Turmell" by Jamin Warren for Kill Screen, May 12, 2011 (https://bit.ly/2UUad1u); "Fireside Chat: Mark Turmell of *NBA Jam* Fame visits SUPER! BitCon 2016" posted by Retro Gamers Society to YouTube, April 12, 2016 (https://youtu.be/aVTxUnLXlYc); "Gamemakers: Boy Wonder" by Dan Gutman in *Electronic Fun with Computer & Games*, vol. 1, no. 1, November 1982 (https://bit.ly/2nfCkKC); and "The GameMakers: The Programmers" by The Feature Creature and The King Fisher for *GamePro* vol. 7, no. 11, November 1995: https://bit.ly/2LkatqW.

Information on *Sneakers*'s release and its sales figures, as well as Marjorie Leeson's comment, are from Greg Voss's "An Interview with Mark Turmell" for *Softline*, vol. 1, no. 2, November 1981: https://bit.ly/2JjxMia. The *People* magazine article on Turmell was called "Invasion of the Vidkids" by Peter Carlson, published February 21, 1983: https://bit.ly/2J4hKZk.

Chapter 4: "He's Heating Up"

Ahmad Rashad's "badly bruised and extremely painful" comment was live commentary during Game 5 of the 1991 NBA Finals: https://youtu.be/FW_-61HsOZE?t=366.

Sales figures on Midway's *Terminator 2: Judgment Day* were provided by George Petro in an interview for this book.

La Guardia's dim view on pinball is documented in Mental Floss's January 25, 2013 article "How Pearl Harbor Led to a War on Pinball" (https://bit.ly/2KUxz47). The figure of 2,500 games destroyed comes from Great Big Story's March 14, 2016 video "When Pinball Was Banned (to Help Win the War)" (https://youtu.be/KeEFkD74hDE).

Gladys Georges's comments to David C. Rudd of the *Chicago Tribune* were reported in "After *Pac-Man*: Video Arcades Today," December 30, 1987: https://bit.ly/2Wnk9Ca.

Information on Patrick Huels's proposed crackdown on arcades in Chicago comes from "Video Game History: 1982 High Tech Rec local news report," uploaded by Duncan F. Brown to YouTube, November 13, 2008: https://youtu.be/7JJywbVZvCI.

Mark Jacobson called West 42nd Street in Times Square "the sleaziest block in America" in "Times Square: a Report From the Sleaziest Block in America," published in the August 6, 1981 issue of *Rolling Stone*.

Chris Bieniek recollects meeting Roger Sharpe in *VideoGames & Computer Entertainment* magazine, issue 61, February 1994: http://bit.ly/2gVeNfW.

NBA Jam's development timeline was partially sourced from Dan Amrich's "*NBA Hangtime*line," which was posted to his website Dan's Mostly *Maximum Hangtime* Shrine: https://bit.ly/300ZPZE.

Chapter 5: "HE'S ON FIRE!"

Details regarding Willie Morris Jr. come from "Air Morris: Lowdown on the High-Flyin' *Jam* Man" by *GamePro* staff for *GamePro's Official NBA Jam Strategy Guide*, 1994.

Details of *NBA Jam*'s development come from "Classic Game Postmortem: *NBA Jam*" by Mark Turmell for GDC 2018, hosted at GDC Vault: https://bit.ly/2UYh4XJ. Details of the game's development were also corroborated with "*NBA Jam* Oral History" by Alex Abnos and Dan Greene for *Sports Illustrated*, April 17, 2017: https://bit.ly/2sHxZAE.

Chapter 6: "BOOMSHAKALAKA!"

"How to WIN at *NBA JAM*!" by Randolph S. Vance, William G. Henderson, and Carl Chavez, first posted to rec.games. video.arcade, is currently available in its August 18, 1993 revised edition at MikesArcade.com (https://bit.ly/2UZRYYu).

Examples of *NBA Jam* slang come from "*JAM TE* Terminology," posted by Michael J. Kokal and Brian L. Smolik to rec.games. video.arcade on June 2, 1994: https://bit.ly/2Y7K7tK.

The cover of *VideoGames & Computer Entertainment*, vol. 5, issue 8 (August 1993) featuring *NBA Jam* (and a screenshot of Kerri Hoskins coming in for a monster jam) can be seen at the Internet Archive: https://bit.ly/2TCQrsa.

Footage captured during the Delta Center's *NBA Jam* Session Video Arcade event can be seen in a February 16, 2019 tweet posted by my @nbajambook account: https://bit.ly/2ZzG8uj.

NBA Jam's reported earnings of $2,468 comes from an earnings audit from mid-July 1993 provided by Mark Turmell: https://imgur.com/a/739JV5v.

The Marcus Webb quote on *NBA Jam*'s week-by-week success was recorded in the *Philadelphia Daily News* in an August 26, 1993 article titled "Game Within a Game: Find the Ringers," written by Curtis Morgan of Knight Ridder Newspapers. Additional information on *NBA Jam*'s place in *RePlay*'s Player's Choice monthly charts comes from an email from Ingird Milkes of *RePlay*.

The Amusement & Music Operators Association naming *NBA Jam* "Most Played Video Game for 1993" and the quote about being "highest earner in the industry's history despite being on the market just eleven months" both come from Mike Conklin's "Contractual Jam Means Games Go On Without Jordan," published in the *Chicago Tribune*, January 11, 1994: https://bit.ly/2OZj3xe.

Stories of the Orlando Magic's love for *NBA Jam* partially come from "Shaq's on fire!" by Jon Robinson for espnW, October 6, 2011. https://es.pn/303kgVQ.

David Robinson being an *NBA Jam* fan comes from "NBA: All-Star Weekend Warriors" by Jon Robinson for ESPN, February 21, 2009: https://es.pn/2vAO6TC.

Chapter 7: "Razzle Dazzle"

Several stories regarding the secrets of *NBA Jam* come from "The Gamer Blog: You don't know *Jam*" by Jon Robinson for ESPN, November 5, 2008: https://es.pn/2IYl7l6.

The text of Stephen E. Liberman's irate letter to Midway management was provided by Mark Turmell. The full text can be seen here: https://imgur.com/a/dHOHD8z.

Eric Kinkead's quote comes from "Judge Dredd - MEGA CITY ONE... IS CROWDED ENOUGH" by Ant Cooke for the website Gaming Hell: https://bit.ly/2IXZKOk.

GamePro editor Dan Amrich's online *NBA Jam* guide (version 1.3 dated April 7, 1994) can be found at GameFAQs: https://bit.ly/2ZRIiCR.

Information on *Jam XXX* comes from two 2012 posts on Nintendo Player: "*NBA Jam XXX* (Prototype, Super Nintendo)" (https://bit.ly/2GTy0JT) and "*NBA Jam XXX*-Posed" (https://bit.ly/2H0t3QU).

Tim Kitzrow speaks to Kotaku in Jason Schreier's "Is This R-Rated Version Of *NBA Jam* Legit? [UPDATE: It's Not, Says Voice Actor]," updated August 6, 2012: https://bit.ly/2NdXYwu.

The July 8, 1993 rec.games.video.arcade post claiming Michael Jordan could be found in the Mall of America cabinet, along with Randolph Vance's response, can be found archived in Google Groups at https://bit.ly/30dXmur.

Mark Turmell's "fast as Spud Webb/good as Pippen" quote comes from Dan Amrich's "Secret Agent Man" in *Slam* magazine #2, October 1994.

Chapter 8: "Jams It In"

Details of Acclaim and its rise come from "Whuppa-Whuppa Whuppa Eeeeeeeeeee! Krrrroooom!" by Charles Platt for *Wired*, June 1, 1995: https://bit.ly/2LizSRP.

The comparison between revenue generated by home games and coin-op games in 1993 comes from Patricia Ann McKanic's March 24, 1994 article, "Video Values: It's a whole new game for the industry," printed in the *Lakeland Ledger*: https://bit.ly/2KDAnU9.

The famous *Mortal Kombat* commercial from 1993 can be seen on YouTube as "*Mortal Kombat* 1 Mortal Monday Commercial by Retroware TV," posted by wwwmortalkombatpl on February 17, 2011: https://youtu.be/R8V7TwlYCt0.

The sales figure of three million copies of *Mortal Kombat* sold comes from an interview with Greg Fischbach for this book.

The *NBA Jam* 45-second commercial can be seen on YouTube as "*NBA Jam* Trailer (1993)," posted May 17, 2015 by Ryan Van Dusen: https://youtu.be/jlNf4vsdXuw.

GamePro's review of the Sega ports appeared in vol. 6, no. 3 (March 1994). The Nintendo Power review of the SNES port appeared in vol. 58 of the same month. *Electronic Gaming*

Monthly's "Better than *Mortal Kombat*?" question was on the cover of vol. 7, issue 2 (February 1994).

News of Acclaim buying Iguana Entertainment and converting it into Acclaim Studios Austin comes from the *New York Times* article "Acclaim to Buy Iguana," December 21, 1994: https://nyti.ms/298jAoO.

Chapter 9: "The Turnover"

Dave Lang and Darryl Wisner of Team GFB Radio's interview with Sal DiVita appeared in "Location Test," episode 33 of their podcast, which originally aired April 24, 2015: https://bit.ly/2JcuRHO.

Pieces of information on the creation of *WWF WrestleMania* come from "*WWF WrestleMania*" by Chris Bieniek for the November 1995 issue of *Tips & Tricks*: https://bit.ly/2WhGaSU.

Denials of Midway cutting ties with Acclaim appeared in the Reuters story "Rumor spurs Acclaim stock fall," published in *Variety* on March 16, 1994: https://bit.ly/2DJuG3m.

Acclaim's press release announcing its exclusive rights to the *NBA Jam* license was distributed February 22, 1995 through Business Wire with the title "Acclaim Launches 'NBA Jam Tournament Edition' on February 23 with Multi-Million Dollar Global Campaign; Company Obtains Worldwide Interactive Rights to 'NBA Jam' Properties."

Information on the disputing stories about the fate of the *NBA Jam* license comes from "A Legal *Jam*" by Dan Amrich for *SLAM*, no. 2, October 1994.

Shawn Liptak's interview with Matt Leone of 1Up.com was published in 2010 as "The Rise, Fall, and Return of *NBA Jam*": https://bit.ly/2UYY7E8.

Josh Smith's review of the Sega Saturn version, "*NBA Jam Extreme* Review," was published on GameSpot May 2, 2000: https://bit.ly/2WhBH2u.

A Reuters report on Dave Mirra suing Acclaim was published in the *Los Angeles Times* on February 15, 2003 as "Cyclist Dave Mirra Sues Game Maker": https://lat.ms/2NdewF4.

Acclaim's publicity stunts have been well documented online. GamesIndustry.biz covered the speeding ticket promotion on October 4, 2002 at the Register as "UK Govt slams 'irresponsible' speed camera refund stunt: Acclaim jumps overboard. Again" (https://bit.ly/31MgdgI). A typical story about the Turok baby name contest can be found in Brian Osborne's "US$10K for your baby's name," published on Geek.com, August 29, 2002 (https://bit.ly/2YWw7rK). Mark Oliver of the *Guardian* covered the headstone story as "Game publicity plan raises grave concerns" on March 15, 2002 (https://bit.ly/2Ze8TfW).

Howard Marks's acquisition of the Acclaim name comes from CRYPTO 101's April 16, 2018 episode, "Activision and Acclaim w/ CEO Howard Marks: Behind the Scenes of 90's

Video Game Companies": https://lnns.co/RvA_MWZPsSw. The subsequent (re)shuttering of Acclaim was covered by Jim Reilly's "Acclaim Closes Down (Again): Online game developer discontinues service," published on IGN.com, June 14, 2012: https://bit.ly/2Z8hmBs.

Information on Acclaim's last days comes from Curt Feldman's August 31, 2004 article "Acclaim shutters offices, staffers ushered off premises" (https://bit.ly/2PNeMtE), as well as his September 2, 2005 article "Former Acclaim boss slammed in court docs" (https://bit.ly/2DPGS2i), both published at GameSpot.

Chapter 10: "The Rebound"

Williams Bally/Midway's "controlling 70 percent of the world market" for pinball comes from Reference for Business's company profile of the parent company WMS Industries, Inc.: https://bit.ly/30bxj75.

Sumner Redstone's 25 percent stake in WMS was reported on April 5, 1994 by David Dishneau in "'Mortal Kombat' Maker to Expand Home Presence With Acquisition," through the Associated Press: https://bit.ly/2Z8oo9n.

Dan Amrich shares an account of Acclaim and Midway's rivalry on display at the May 1996 Electronic Entertainment Expo in his "*NBA Hangtime*line."

NBA Hangtime's flyer with "the original *NBA Jam* design team" tagline can be found at the Arcade Flyer Archive: https://bit.ly/2YRTQt8.

NBA Hangtime sales figures of about 15,000 cabinets come directly from Mark Turmell and Sal DiVita in an interview for this book.

Details of *NFL Blitz*'s development come from "How In The Hell Did *NFL Blitz* Ever Get Made?" by Aaron Gordon for VICE Sports, November 6, 2014: https://bit.ly/2UZTh9X.

Mark Turmell and Sal DiVita talk *NFL Blitz* with Jon Robinson, a.k.a. "Johnny Ballgame" in the article "Hot at the Arcades: *NFL Blitz*", published in *GamePro* issue 108, September 1997: https://bit.ly/2E1kqDR. Jon Robinson later recalled *NFL Blitz*'s debut in an ESPN article, "Five things to know about *NFL Blitz*," published October 20, 2011: https://es.pn/2Yf9KsV. Sales figures of roughly 13,000 units were estimated by Turmell and DiVita in an interview for this book.

Bruce Headlam reports Williams's closure of the pinball operations in "Pinball Line Closing Down," published in the *New York Times*, Oct. 28, 1999: https://nyti.ms/2Mncx1c.

The March 6, 2001 press release announcing the reduction of 60 employees ("about 8% of the Company's total employee base") was released by Business Wire with the title "Midway Games Reduces Coin-op Overhead." News from the subsequent June 22, 2001 press release was reported that same day by Yahoo! Finance as "Midway Games to exit coin-op video game market" (https://bit.ly/349JQKG).

Chapter 11: "The Nail In The Coffin"

Jeremy Horwitz's "Mortal Apathy?" was published July 8, 2002 in the *New York Times*: https://nyti.ms/2GY51ET. This article also provides information on Midway's forecasted losses of $10 million—and then $12.5 million—as well as *Mortal Kombat: Deadly Alliance*'s delayed release.

The figure of $116 million lost by Midway in 2003 comes from their annual report for that year, hosted at the Internet Archive: https://bit.ly/30LJwzD.

Information on RenderWare comes from interviews with Mark Turmell for this book. Eric Bangeman reports on how "EA gets exclusive rights to the NFL" in Ars Technica, December 13, 2004: https://bit.ly/2z6DHk5.

Steve Allison's comments on *Blitz: The League* can be found in Rob Fahey's December 17, 2004 article "Midway plans unlicensed American Football title," published at GamesIndustry.biz: https://bit.ly/2MnKKOb.

Fear & Respect was featured on the cover of *Game Informer* issue 141 (January 2005).

The story of Neil Nicastro's resignation was reported by Andrew Countryman in the *Chicago Tribune*'s June 5, 2004 article, "Midway Games chairman to resign": https://bit.ly/2VbUtM5.

Information on Sumner Redstone as a majority shareholder in Midway in late 2007 comes from Kris Graft's "Midway

Creditors Sue Redstones, Board Members Over Sale Of Company," published May 13, 2009 at Gamasutra (https://ubm.io/2HbkO45). News of his 87 percent stake in the company was reported in Tor Thorsen's December 2, 2008 GameSpot article "Redstone dumps Midway for $100K" (https://bit.ly/2Z3IgeJ). More information on Redstone's stock dump comes from Melissa Marr's December 1, 2008 *Wall Street Journal* article "Redstone Sells Control of Midway to Ease Debt" (https://on.wsj.com/2KCIxMw).

Information on John Romeo's involvement in *Gauntlet: Seven Sorrows* comes from "Romero exits Midway" by Tor Thorsen for GameSpot, July 14, 2005: https://bit.ly/2GWgFQm.

Matt Booty's comments on Midway filing for bankruptcy were reported in Brian Crecente's February 12, 2009 Kotaku article "Midway Files for Bankruptcy": https://bit.ly/2MlPqnB.

Tor Thorsen's July 16, 2009 GameSpot article "Midway's Chicago HQ closing, final buyout price $49 million" covers the auctioning off of Midway's assets to Warner Bros.: https://bit.ly/2OZ2Ec9. An example of midway.com redirecting to warnerbros.com can be observed in a snapshot from February 5, 2010 available at the Internet Archive: https://bit.ly/2Z5gGwN.

Chapter 12: "Launches A Shot"

Several details in this chapter come from "*NBA JAM* 2010 - Bringing Back the BOOMSHAKALAKA!" by Trey Smith at GDC 2011, hosted at GDC Vault: https://bit.ly/2DLFg9P.

Steve Thomason praises *NBA Jam* for the Wii in "Boom Shakalaka!", published in *Nintendo Power* issue 251 (February 2010). Griffin McElroy's October 5, 2010 Joystiq review "*NBA Jam* review: Make new modes, but keep the old" can be found hosted at Engadget: https://engt.co/2ZcpdOu.

USA Today's Mike Snider interviewed Trey Smith and Mark Turmell in "President dunks in 'NBA Jam'," published October 5, 2010. Kotaku's Owen Good reports on Peter Moore's appearance on Fox News in "Fox News Wonders If *NBA Jam* Is A Truly Bipartisan Game," published October 7, 2010: https://bit.ly/2KCZYwp.

News of *NBA Jam* being a free downloadable bundled with *NBA Elite 11* was reported by Dave Rudden in the August 3, 2010 Network Word article "*NBA Jam* coming to 360/PS3 free with *NBA Elite* download August 3, 2010": https://bit.ly/2HcFF6Y.

Lee Bradley reported on the February 12, 2014 @nbajam tweet in his article "EA Hinting at New *NBA Jam* Game Announcement," published at Xbox Achievements the following day (https://bit.ly/2KOSQw1). A day later on February 14, Bradley followed up on the story with "*NBA Jam* Tease the Result of 'Unauthorised Use' of Twitter Account" (https://bit.ly/2Z1hm7e).

Sales figures of *NBA Jam*'s Android port and its success on the PlayStation Store comes from an interview with Trey Smith for this book.

Chapter 13: "Swish"

The attendance figure of "18,000" for the March 19, 2015 Denver Nuggets at Houston Rockets game comes from Basketball Reference: https://bit.ly/2YYgS1p. The precise figure was 18,456.

Game Informer magazine counts down their top 300 games of all time in their 300th issue, published April 2018.

News of Scientific Games Corporation buying WMS Gaming reported in the October 18, 2013 press release "Scientific Games Completes Acquisition Of WMS," available from Cision PR Newswire: https://prn.to/2YVrxdq.

Bubble Safari's success was reported in Eric Caoili's June 12, 2012 Gamasutra article "Fastest-growing Facebook games: From *Bubble Safari* to *Song Pop*": https://ubm.io/33yLdSS.

ACKNOWLEDGEMENTS

When Boss Fight Books accepted my pitch for this book in June 2015, my life was in a different place. I was engaged, childless, and lived in an apartment. My familiarity with *NBA Jam* was limited. I knew a few things, sure, but certainly not enough to flesh out an entire book. I figured the project would necessitate a dozen interviews, and I'd be done within a year, maybe two.

As I write these last words in April 2019, I'm a homeowner, a husband, and a father. At this moment, I would bet that I know more about *NBA Jam* and the culture surrounding the game than anyone else on the planet. Completing this book has put more professional and personal challenges in front of me than any other project, but I'm deeply grateful to have had the chance to spend years talking and thinking about something that I and so many others love so much.

NBA Jam (the book) has made an indelible impact on my life, in some ways more surprising than others. In 2018, on the morning of March 22—one of the most crucial dates in the mythology of *NBA Jam*—I sent Mark Turmell a happy birthday text. At 4:54 p.m., my daughter Catalina Ahmed Ali was born, three weeks ahead of schedule. That night, Turmell was the one texting me well-wishes.

This book, as it exists, would have not been possible with the generous time and insight of the many people I interviewed and corresponded with. Chiefly, thanks go out to Brian Colin, Chris Bieniek, Dan Amrich, David Crane, Eric Samulski, Eugene Jarvis, George Clinton, George Petro, Glen Rice, Greg Fischbach, Greg Lassen, Ingrid Milkes, J. Moon, Jamie Rivett, Jeff Nauman, Jeffrey Allen Townes, Jim Greene, John Carlton, John Newcomer, John Romero, John Root, John Tobias, Jon Hey, Jon Robinson, Josh Tsui, Kenneth Faried, Kerri Ann Hoskins Reavis, Lorraine Hocker, Mark Turmell, Matt Booty, Michele Brown, Nolan Bushnell, Paul Samulski, Randolph Vance, Roger Sharpe, Sal DiVita, Sam Goldberg, Sarah Cocchiola, Shaquille O'Neal, Shawn Liptak, Stephen Howard, Tim Kitzrow, and Trey Smith. During the development of this book, J. Moon and William "Greg" Henderson passed away. They are deeply missed.

This book would also not exist without Gabe Durham and Michael P. Williams, who have been nothing but supportive as this project has grown and changed from my initial vision. I'm appreciative of both the opportunity and your belief in the value of *NBA Jam*'s story, and for all the time you gave me. Thanks also to Ken Baumann and Cory Schmitz for their work on the cover, Christopher Moyer for layout,

Ryan Plummer for copyediting, and Nick Sweeney and Joseph M. Owens for proofreading. Thanks to Evan Nixon for his fantastic promotional artwork. Thanks to the many Kickstarter backers, Twitter users, and other advocates who have supported me through this arduous process.

Thanks to the many inspirations who have fueled me on this marathon, especially author David Kushner and his sensational book *Masters of Doom: How Two Guys Created an Empire and Transformed Pop Culture.*

Looking back further, thanks to all of my English teachers over the years for their support and guidance; in particular, thanks to Michelle Feige and professor Dennis Read. Thanks to the many editors of alt-weeklies, magazines, and sites that I worked with over the years for all the assignments and advice.

Thanks to Derek Styer, Jeremiah Santos, Joey Peters, Terrence Tuy, and the great friends whom I have confided in closely during this project. Thanks to Justin Deering, Kehneth Yeung, and Michael Kalnins, friends who doubled as editors, and Jon Mann for inspiring the opening of this book's pitch. Thanks to the many friends at Smart Harbor and The Shipyard for all the support.

Thanks to my parents, Sarah Blotner and Deed Ahmed Ali, who have been down since day one. For their decades of support and love, thanks to my incredible family members: among many others, Ben Blotner, David Hill, Eram Ahmed Ali, Judy Hill, Najdah Khan, Nazli Jafri, Orooj Ahmed Ali, Phyllis and José Prats, and

Shahana Ahmed Ali. Thanks and love to my brother in everything but blood, Kazi Nur-ul-Islam.

Thanks to my late grandfathers Professor Ahmed Ali and Dr. Robert Sherman Hill, both of whom served as invaluable inspirations and influences over my whole life. I wish you were here to see this.

Lastly, a special thanks to my wife Elia for having my back every step of the way during this long, long process. I'm grateful for your patience, support, and sacrifices through the ups and downs. You're an extraordinary person. I can finally, truthfully say: *It's finished*. I knew it would take me a minute.

This moment takes me back to being a kid in Karachi, Pakistan in the 90s, which was where I fell in love with American pop culture and imagined contributing something of my own to it someday. Once a month, a family member would take me to Say Publishing to get a video game magazine, and it would be a special occasion. I would get to buy one magazine a month, two or more if I was lucky. Reading about games gave me such a rush; being able to write a book about one of the best is even better. I always pictured speaking to you from my own pages, and here we are.

It was all a dream.

SPECIAL THANKS

For making our fourth season of books possible, Boss Fight Books would like to thank Cathy Durham, Edwin Locke, Nancy Magnusson-Durham, Ken Durham, Yoan Sebdoun-Manny, Tom Kennedy, Guillaume Mouton, Peter Smith, Mark Kuchler, Corey Losey, David Litke, James Terry, Patrick King, Nicole Kline, Seth Henriksen, Devin J. Kelly, Eric W. Wei, John Simms, Daniel Greenberg, Jennifer Durham-Fowler, Neil Pearson, Maxwell Neely-Cohen, Todd Hansberger, Chris Furniss, Jamie Perez, Joe Murray, and Mitchel Labonté.

ALSO FROM
BOSS FIGHT BOOKS